STANDING OUT FROM THE CROWD

To my long-time friends Tony & Sue Alexandra, with warmest regards,

[signature]

Executive Books

Standing Out From The Crowd

Differentiating Yourself and All You Offer
in a Competitive World

Published by:
Executive Books

1-800-233-2665
www.executivebooks.com

ISBN: 978-1-949033-15-1

Printed in the United States of America

DEDICATION

It is with heartfelt memories and total reverence that I dedicate this book to the life of my friend of 45 years, mentor and colleague, Charlie "Tremendous" Jones. His impact on my faith, my career, my reading habits and my competencies has been inestimable. The late Charlie "Tremendous" Jones indeed, stood out from the crowd!

ACKNOWLEDGEMENTS

First, I would like to thank U. S. Learning's Marketing SVP, Bob Carroll. He helped immensely in putting this book together. Also, my assistant, Betty Johnson, who was on hand to do whatever we needed to make progress on the project.

Our CIO at U. S. Learning, Terri Murphy, made meaningful contributions to the ideas in the book, especially as related to Social media, for which I offer my thanks.

Special thanks to my co-author of The One Minute Entrepreneur, Dr. Ken Blanchard, for his influence on my desire and passion to keep writing. I consider him my Publishing Mentor.

I wish to express thanks and gratitude to my colleagues with whom I have had the pleasure of learning, researching, and teaching the Behavioral Style concept: Dr. David Merrill, Larry Wilson, Don Thoren, Dr. Paul Green and Dr. Tony Alessandra.

I also acknowledge the expertise and professionalism of Tracey Jones, CEO of Executive Books/Tremendous Life Books and her team for bringing the book to life with their extraordinary publishing expertise.

Last but not least, I want to thank my colleagues in our think tank, Speakers Roundtable, for their significant influence on my thinking and my expertise, and their continuing influence on my desire to research and create new material and meaningful content.

TABLE OF CONTENTS

STANDING OUT FROM THE CROWD

Introduction

STANDING OUT FROM THE CROWD

Whether you are a sales representative for a manufacturer, an internet marketer, or a retail entrepreneur, your industry or specialized space does not need another "Me Too" performer. Whatever you do, try to be the best in your business! This book is structured to provide a separate track to run on that will distinguish you from others in today's crowded marketplace.

The Latin term, "Sui Generis", means 'one of a kind'. That's what you need to be in your business – a *one-off*, innovative problem solver, who has developed a reputation for being exceptional. Can you become so good that you can make your competition irrelevant? I think you can and I want to help.

Nobody can be you! Nobody else on the planet is just like you. We all need to recognize the power of individuality and leverage the skills we have amassed to be exceptional. For some, individuality is the most outstanding asset possessed. We should develop uniqueness in every manner to be able to impress people with our attention to detail, relevance, and the means by which we tailor and deliver solutions. If we can do those things well, we are destined to gain market share and amass wealth in the process.

This book is divided into five parts to give a broad perspective on how you can be perceived as different from—and superior to,—your competition. Your image of yourself, your product, or your company is not a constant; it is an ever-changing variable. Over time we need to make as many positive deposits in our "Reputation Bank" as possible, by delivering exceptional products, differentiated offerings, or "knock-their-socks-off" service!

This 5-part, 34-chapter book is based on many years of personal research. In an effort to make it more rewarding, I have added references to videos that will help reinforce the points I am making. As you read, you will notice links to these short video clips. Take time to review them and gain additional ideas on the implementation of skills discussed.

In *Standing Out From The Crowd*, do not assume I want you to feel so special that you counterproductively create a huge ego for yourself. My old friend, Zig Ziglar, was right when he advised, "Don't contract the disease of Egomania – it makes everybody sick except the one who has got it!" Let's be adaptable to the needs of those we serve, and display humility in the process, and we will earn the right to be referred to by our clients as a "Trusted Advisor".

You will gain many ideas from this book. Carefully consider them and decide which to adopt as core competencies on your way to great success. I sincerely hope this book helps you significantly in crafting your path to becoming the unsurpassed, one of a kind, extraordinary producer who does indeed *stand out from the crowd*.

Don Hutson

PART I

DIFFERENTIATING YOURSELF AND ALL YOU OFFER

PREMISE

Giving in-depth thought to how you plan to "Go to Market", with unique elements different from your competitors, is a huge step in the right direction. If you sell a commodity, it may be challenging, but it is certainly worth your effort

The elements of differentiation you incorporate into your offerings will often be the key to *standing out from the crowd*. The differentiation model I developed

STANDING OUT FROM THE CROWD has eight types, each of which could be the very thing you need to be able to tell the marketplace of your uniqueness and why they should do business with you over everyone else.

Chapter 1

STANDING OUT FROM THE CROWD!

My favorite question to ask sales professionals and entrepreneurs is "How are your offerings different from, and better than, those of your competitors?" Anytime I get a response like, "Well… Uh……" I know I am talking to someone in big trouble. The key to gaining market share and prospering in today's competitive environment is to differentiate yourself, your company, and your offerings as distinctively and creatively as you can. You need to *stand out from the crowd!*

My second favorite question to ask them is "How many of your differentiators represent ways you are personally distinctive and creative in serving your customers and providing them with solutions?"

Many people think there are only two types of differentiation: product and price. That shallow perspective will not advance your effort to gain market share and outperform the competition. Neither your product nor your price encompasses your personal service, the effort you put forth to help them solve their problem, or the creativity with which you involve your team members in creating a solution for them. So please don't go to market thinking you must have the absolute best product or the absolute lowest price to win! There is so much more to it than that.

Our U.S. Learning model is made up of eight types of differentiation. The thoughtful consideration of each, including ideas from brainstorming with your colleagues, can assist you in creating a platform for winning more business than ever. Here's a list of the eight with definitions:

1. Product Differentiation – There will be times in your career when you are offering a truly superior product. When the stars align and this happens, make hay while the sun shines! Always push for superior product development! It can often

be inspired by a customer who is articulating a new need.

2. Experiential Differentiation – When was the last time you did something that made your customer say "Wow!"? Many today believe we are in an "experience economy" where the mundane transaction falls far behind a dynamic service experience. This is the service side of selling. When you can amaze and delight a customer it will propel you to (or closer to) the top of their preferred vendor list!

3. Relationship Differentiation – If you have done a fine job of developing a relationship with a given prospect or client, it might give you the edge over your immediate competitors. People still want to do business with people they know, like, and trust. The relationship can make or break any deal, so give each one your best effort!

4. Process Differentiation – This is how you and your company

do what you do. Do you have creative processes of doing business that separate you from the crowd? One of the best things you can do to make and keep customers happy is to take the pain out of their life! Put processes in place that delight your customers and make you easy to do business with.

5. Marketing Differentiation – All other things being equal, if your marketing process is superior, you have a good shot at securing the business! Marketing has typically been perceived as sales, public relations, and advertising. In today's world of business development, it should also include social media. If you can outsell your competition, you win!

6. Technological Differentiation – How is the solution you are offering technologically superior to the competition? When you do your needs-analysis ask what features or benefits could revolutionize products in your

space. Push the envelope in coming up with technological advances that will give you a competitive edge. It may be your prospect's idea, or your Director of Product Development's invention or advancement, but you can be the facilitator to bring it about. If the distinction is not about the product itself, technological differentiation could be about the means and methods of communication you deploy.

7. Social Media Differentiation – If all other things are comparable, when compared to a competitor, your social media skills and the programs you have used to stay in touch with your customers in a meaningful manner are more important than ever! And, they can even be the *dealmaker*...or *dealbreaker*.

8. Price Differentiation – This is when you either have the lowest price or (more generally) the best value proposition. I believe there is more opportunity to

sell value rather than cut price!
Tap the "collective intellect" of
your team members and decide
the most advantageous manner
to go to market!

Remember, differentiation offers
you the advantage you need to continue
gaining market share and prospering in
today's competitive environment. Be creative! Find unique ways to differentiate
yourself, your company, and all you offer
as distinctively as you can.

Follow these guidelines regarding differentiation and you will always *stand out
from the crowd!*

Chapter 2

WINNING SALES BATTLES WITH PRODUCT DIFFERENTIATION!

Product Differentiation represents both *opportunities* and *challenges*.

One *challenge* is how to overcome a defeatist mindset when you are selling anything—especially a commodity. Many in this area subscribe to the philosophy that a commodity is what it is, and we are all selling the *same* thing to the *same* market. So, we had better be the cheapest or we are not going to get any orders. Change your thinking!

One *opportunity* is to get creative and figure out a way to go to market with offers that outshine those of your competitors.

How can we go to market selling a commodity without a comparable offer?

The offer encompasses more than the commoditized product itself, so get your smartest folks together to brainstorm how you can make your offer different.

Here are some ideas:

1. Six Months Same as Cash – If you can fine-tune your offer to include a more favorable payment plan, you will have a market advantage;

2. Buy One Ton or More and get 20 Widgets Free! – This is the "Comp Add-on". Buy your add-on (that they want) at a modest price and gain a market advantage.

3. Appropriate Gifting – Come up with a series of promotional products your buyers like, and need, that feature your company's logo. Then, make certain that they get these utilitarian sales support items on, at least, a quarterly basis. Be innovative! Discover things no one else has thought of. This can help cement awareness of you and your company in the minds

of your customers. Years ago, I bought 500 small pop-up note-holders with my name and contact information on it. These holders were handy and useful, and I actually had a few clients tell me they think of me daily! Some still use the noteholders after 15 or 20 years!

4. Usurp the Commodity Label – Is there a way your company can tweak or improve your product in a manner that de-commoditizes it? For example, producing it with one unique component that weighs less than the normal one, thus decreasing shipping costs. I have clients whose "thought pioneers" have made things like this happen! *This is true product differentiation.* Hopefully you have some "hot brains" in your company who can create such unique products and market them aggressively. But, time is of the essence, when your competitors see how well your unique product approaches are

working, they may very well try to reverse engineer them to enhance their position before you know it!

5. Special Events – Invite the top 20% of your customers (who are probably responsible for 80% of your business) to a special fundraising event your company has staged to raise money for a worthwhile charity. Events of this type are often attended by VIPs with whom everyone wants to associate. When your company makes this kind of an event part of an ongoing effort, your offer can be better received by the marketplace.

Will all of these work in your case? Maybe and maybe *not*. That's where your creativity comes into play. Take these examples to your marketing team and use them as "thought starters" as you implement outstanding ways to stay relevant in the minds of the decision-makers in your universe.

Be prepared to step up to the *challenges* that confront professionals in highly competitive sales situations. Be resourceful! Seize the *opportunities* you discover that can be the key to making product differentiation work well for you!

Chapter 3

Experiential Differentiation: The Miracle of Out-Serving Your Competition

Experiential Differentiation is the unique way you perform services for your clients. Think about it for a minute. Do you and your team members give them an experience to remember, as opposed to just good service? If j*ust good service* is what most everybody else provides (only enough to get by), experiential differentiation can be your secret sales weapon. The "Bar of Excellence" in terms of customer satisfaction is higher today than ever before. We need to determine we are going to remain at the top, in comparison to similar product and service providers, by truly differentiating ourselves from the competition.

Since our goal is to make clients happy with the way we work – and to keep them that way – let's explore the tactical side of service delivery. To demonstrate exceptional interpersonal skills, we need to display the following eight behaviors when one-on-one with customers:

- Greet them with a sincere smile—in person and on the phone.

- Maintain good eye contact coupled with exceptional listening skills.

- Exhibit a can-do spirit.

- Provide efficient responses.

- Apologize when appropriate.

- Ask what else you can do to enhance their satisfaction.

- Use their name.

- Thank them and invite them to reconnect the next time they need your brand of service.

What if one of your top ten biggest customers used the A-F grading scale to rate you, and your top four competitors, in multiple service areas like:

a. Creative solutions to problems

b. Prompt response to inquiries

c. On-time order delivery and price accuracy

d. No-hassle relationship skills

e. Exceptional telephone skills

How would you and your colleagues stack up? If you do a deep dive to see how you could achieve exceptional performance in these areas, you will have a good idea about your level of experiential differentiation. You will also have a very useful report card you can use as a guide to adding any improvements required to maintain – and expand – your competitive advantage.

In their excellent book, *The Experience Economy*, Pine and Gilmore elaborate on the power and potential of creating exceptional service experiences to impress customers and gain loyalty. This merits out-of-the-box thinking on your part and uncompromising support from your management team! This can also serve as an additional boost to your goal of dominance in a competitive market. The edge you gain can make a significant difference.

If you want to benefit from the *Graduate Course* in providing exceptional experiences, you must position yourself to perform periodic "customer service miracles". This can happen when you make client service excellence your primary goal. You have to be looking for the opportunities. When one presents itself, seize it! A client service miracle is something that, when performed, makes clients say "WOW!" If you are not looking for these opportunities, they will be whizzing by your head all week long. People love great service and exceptional experiences where they do business.

I recommend you
view this video clip:

**"Customer Service
Miracles"**

https://vimeo.com/268729319

Chapter 4

RELATIONSHIP DIFFERENTIATION: YOUR PATH TO *TRUSTED ADVISOR* STATUS!

One of the greatest opportunities you have in business today is mastering the principles of Relationship Differentiation, which can put you on the road to gaining Trusted Advisor status. It can propel you to the top of your prospect's list of vendors in your marketplace.

You simply want to develop a more compelling and collaborative relationship with your prospects, than your competitors, and here are fourteen elements to get you there:

1. Establish a list of your Top 100 prospects or clients and focus your time and energy on them.

2. Increase your focus and efforts on the VALUE each of your prospects and clients care about. (It may vary substantially from person to person.)

3. Subscribe to the premise, "When we care about our clients' outcomes as much, or more, as we do our own, we will be totally trusted."

4. Gain expertise which demonstrates that you have earned the right to enjoy Trusted Advisor status. Staying educated on the latest and best practices is critical.

5. Display unquestionable integrity in all dealings to assure that your reputation is stellar.

6. Link the needs and priorities of your clients or prospects to yours for *win-win* outcomes.

7. Learn all you can about your Top 100 prospects and clients, so that you can better know how to serve them.

8. Stay in touch at appropriate intervals, communicating with them in their preferred manner.

9. Let them know you are thinking of them by sending them items of interest (articles, blogs, and other information) they could find helpful.

10. Refer them business when you can. Few things are appreciated more.

11. Introduce them to someone who you think might develop into a treasured contact for them over time.

12. Sponsor them into an organization you belong to that might help them and their business.

13. Do something meaningful for one of their kids.

14. Target a select person you would like to have as a "confidant" and engage with them on a personal and business basis.

As you read over the elements of the above 14 recommendations, you may want to fine-tune them for a better fit with your selling style or prospect base. The key is to be exceptional by doing things that most people either never think to do—or are not inclined to do. Only by walking in the shoes of our prospects and clients can we learn what they value and how we can be most helpful to them. To be able to walk in their shoes, we must be expert information-collectors. We can only achieve that through the skill of asking thoughtful questions and exercising our skill of active listening. When Ken Blanchard and I wrote, *The One Minute Entrepreneur*, we advanced the idea that those most talented in relationship development were the professionals who led with their ears! Do it! It *works*.

Chapter 5

PROCESS DIFFERENTIATION: YOUR BEST RESPONSE TO A COMPETITOR'S PRICE-ONLY POSITION

In our continuing effort to present commonsense ideas on how you can be unique in your marketplace, this chapter will cover *Process Differentiation, or how* you do *what* you do in a way that makes you unique in your marketplace.

I'll give you an example. Recently, at the Atlantis Hotel in Nassau, Bahamas, I conducted a *Selling Value Seminar* for a large plastics company which manufactures shopping bags for grocers, department stores, and other retailers.

This seminar was billed as their annual *Customers Council Trip*. The bags they manufacture are of high quality, but still considered "commodity" products. This compelling customer event represents their *Process Differentiation* since they are the only company among their peers who host such a top-notch outing.

Their customers bring their spouses to be a part of these meetings that are held at luxurious venues. This gives the company's executives and sales professionals the opportunity to spend high-quality time with and hear from their customers in a very pleasant environment. The customers really appreciate the trip and, of course, the company gains enhanced customer allegiance, which is critical in their ultra-competitive "commodity" product environment.

What is your process of doing business? Are there things you could do which would help you or your company be perceived as exceptional in some way? When we don't push the envelope to find ways to display our unique approach to doing business, we tend to perpetuate the image of just another company that sells commodities. Here are some additional "thought starters" for you and your company to consider trying, in order to be perceived as *exceptional* rather than *just another vendor*.

1. When you have a prospective buyer who openly expresses discontent with you or your industry's products as being basic and uncreative, inquire about his/her special needs or suggestions as to what he/she would do to make things better. Perhaps that buyer is open and comfortable enough with you to say *"If your people could figure out a way to engineer 5% off the weight of these products, I'd be eager to buy from you"*. A viable way to combat commoditization is to de-commoditize your product in a meaningful way!

2. What if you and your colleagues could figure out a way to get the products to customers faster? What if your new policy is to ship via overnight carrier for faster delivery when the rest of your industry is shipping via a truck line? Perhaps

your increased shipping cost will be more than offset by an increase in market share, representing a net gain.

3. What if your company created a point system (like frequent flier miles for example) that serves as a device to de-commoditize your offering and create advantages for them over time?

Perhaps none of the above is perfect for your organization, but the examples shown can certainly stimulate new ideas and logic paths in a strategy meeting of sales and marketing innovators at your company. I suggest that you think outside of the box to identify how you can use *Process Differentiation* to creatively enhance your delivery system so that you are not at the mercy of price.

Chapter 6

AN AWESOME ADVANTAGE FOR YOU: MARKETING DIFFERENTIATION

When everything you and your competitors offer customers is basically equal, a superior marketing approach can win the business for you. So, what does a superior marketing approach look like in today's ever-changing marketplace?

For starters, your company's *traditional* marketing approach should be empowered by first-rate sales, advertising, public relations, and promotional methods and materials that generate an aura of value about your products and services from your customers' perspectives.

The other prime component of a modern marketing approach is the integration of *web-based initiatives* into the implementation of the plan. Anyone who does not include internet marketing and social media in the mix today is short-sighted, since effective command of this incredible resource will be a difference-maker – *now and from now on!*

Two issues come into play on each differentiating factor; your uniqueness and your offering's relevance to each customer. And the perception and appeal of each can vary widely from customer to customer based largely on five elements. Let's cover these one at a time.

Advertising – Is your company building a solid brand and reputation with advertising that is positively impacting, creative, and appealing to your customer base? If the sales and marketing team at your company can ascertain what the top five "value points" are that cause people to buy from you, they will have a strong basis for ad development that will capture the attention of your prospective buyers and cause them to take action – *in your favor*. William Wrigley of chewing gum fame, was known to have said "Half of my advertising spend is wasted; *I just don't know which half.*" Today we have the ability to measure key metrics in a more viable manner to appropriately target the right people.

Promotional – Does your company periodically offer special promotions, coupons, or "sales" that compel your customers to buy more or try new or updated items? If not, you may want to give it a try to gain new revenues and more of a following from people who have not been compelled to buy these items from you previously. It can be a tool for increased market penetration. But, be careful not to sabotage previously top-selling items in your line in the process. I advise my clients to form marketing committees who can get together to brainstorm options. The collective intellect of those from multiple disciplines within any company can come together to formulate solid, creative promotional approaches.

Public Relations – What kinds of messages are you sending through press releases and special notices, and in the case of larger companies, your annual report letter, that might positively impact your sales? What kind of grade do you give your company on finding excellent ways to inform the marketplace of your latest and most advanced products, services, and customer support technologies? In most industries, customers are becoming more discerning and competition is getting keener than ever, so go after every market advantage you can through well thought out PR.

Sales – Do your sales team members' skills exceed those of your top competitors? You will either be at an advantage or disadvantage in this regard, so management's commitment to provide the sales team with the best, up to date, quality sales training is key for gaining—*and maintaining*—the advantage.

Are you using outdated sales techniques and approaches that evoke resistance rather than acceptance? *"Always be closing"* is a concept that should be eliminated from your company's vocabulary! Whenever possible, a *win-win*, collaborative approach is preferred. That way, you are more likely to get the order today and build a bridge to future business.

Social Media – How are you different from and better than your competitors in this vital area? When you learn to harness the incredible power of social media, this awesome technology can easily become the game-changer for you. Disregard this potential, and you risk losing ground in your marketplace to competitors whose advanced digital presence outshines yours! (See more on this topic in Chapter 9).

Chapter 7

AN EXCITING OPPORTUNITY: TECHNOLOGICAL DIFFERENTIATION

This era of technological advancement is one that stimulates the mind of all observers. We never know what is coming next! It is incumbent upon all of us to sort through these advancements to identify what represents opportunity for us as marketers, sales professionals, and business communicators.

Members of academia tell us that the knowledge mass of the human race is doubling approximately every four years. It is undeniable that levels of technological progress are exponentially greater than that and increasing every day. What can we do to assure that we will be able to capitalize on all of it rather than become a victim?

The opportunities I see in this arena are technological advances in the development and manufacture of our products or services, technological improvement in the delivery of our products and services, and the improvement of technology enabling us to communicate better and more proficiently with our prospects and clients.

Is your company fully investigating the potential of technological advances in these three areas?

Are you fully evaluating the latest technological potential of all interactive opportunities? Are you using video to communicate with your clients? Have you thought about trying *BombBomb*, which enables you to send a video message captured on your laptop camera via email to get your message to your prospects and clients with improved engagement? Or, how about *Zoom*, which gives you additional capabilities with the video medium (enabling recording of the content of both sides of a conversation in which you are a participant as long as you advise other parties involved in the conversation in advance as to what you are doing)? Are Twitter, Facebook, or LinkedIn outlets that you regularly use or just something you hear about others using?

An audience member in a seminar recently asked, "Don, what is the best way to communicate with a client?" I responded, "I'm not the best one to ask. Ask your clients!" Learn from them the methods of communications each prefers and use them – *proficiently!* The status quo of yesterday's communication methods could well take us into a downward spiral through mediocrity and into oblivion!

Here are 5 elements in determining our communications platforms with clients and prospects:

1. Review your communication initiatives and determine if you can benefit from some diversity. If you are only using email campaigns, consider adding the power of texting too. *HeyWire Messenger* reports an email can get lost in an overcrowded inbox, while the average text message is opened and read within 3 minutes. This is especially important with Millennials.

2. If you don't get a response after several emails, mix up the medium by using a video email to create a more transparent and personal connection.

3. Don't rely just on email or text. Pick up the phone! Studies have proven that phone calls, leaving a compelling message, can provide a higher response rate than direct mail alone.

4. Also, determine when it is most advisable to make an actual visit. It shows initiative and makes a positive impression that you desire a business relationship with them.

5. Avoid sending email when you really need face to face communications. Issues like price changes and contract amendments may be better served face to face.

So, the key is to find the proper balance with each person; one that works for them and works for you. Learn their preferences and expand your technological capabilities so you can beat your competition with an effective communications flow.

Consider technology your friend! It will open doors, keep relationships glued, and, when used to the fullest and most creative extent, give you a competitive edge!

Chapter 8

SOCIAL MEDIA DIFFERENTIATION

Social Media Differentiation is the seventh type of differentiation in our model. What grade (A, B, C, D, or F) would you give yourself on your skill and engagement of social media? If all other things are equal when compared to a competitor, your social media footprint and skills—coupled with the programs you have used to stay in touch with your customers in a meaningful manner—are more important than ever! And, they can even be the deal-maker...or deal-*breaker*.

Let's take a micro and a macro look at social media strategies and how you can more effectively penetrate your market.

First, the big picture... Have you recently developed a "profile of your perfect customer"? Please do so for putting your best foot forward in prospecting for new business via social media.

This would include typical age range, level of education, and other attributes of those who have benefitted the most from your products or services in the past. The more detail the better. As you develop your perfect customer profile, you will be able to formulate decisions on how to best use social media to contact them and stay in touch inoffensively.

A closer look at each prospect individually will help even more. During a conversation with them, simply ask *"Which social media programs do you regularly use?"* Then, communicate with them via their preferred format.

As you compete in a tough marketplace, being "top of mind" among your prospects and clients is key. To improve your digital footprint and promote engagement, here are 5 "Do's and Don'ts":

1. Don't assume you need to be on all social media channels. Do your homework and determine where your expertise and specialty will be most relevant.

2. Don't just post for the sake of being "on" social media. What is the purpose for sharing your

expertise? Are you looking to stay connected for ongoing sales opportunities? If so, then regular posts by you can help position you as their "celebrity authority". When you have an end objective in mind, you are better positioned to develop a comprehensive editorial and marketing calendar. Using this as your guide for publication dates, you can offer rich content that is aligned and focused on clear outcomes that can generate more sales and customer retention for you and your business.

3. Define what your ultimate goal is from the investment of your time. What are the outcomes you are seeking? Are you looking to present your product or service to companies? Then target companies. If you are looking to get a consulting job, then posting 3 or 5 strategies may be the ticket to prompt the next step in getting potential clients

to contact you for more information.

4. Consider "purposeful posting". Launch your editorial and marketing calendar with a goal to study and monitor where you get the most responses. Note what content was used and on what channels your postings promoted the most meaningful engagement required to build a community of fans with your ultimate goal in mind.

5. Post with a value-added link to encourage the next step for engagement. If you are posting several tips or initiatives, offer a link to a free, more detailed downloadable report from your website, or a video link that drives traffic to your website or YouTube channel. When you set up the link with a "lead capture" feature, you can monitor and measure the response.

Be aware that building a community requires attention, measurement, and monitoring. It's not a quick fix, but it can, with consistent effort, change the significance of your following, and thus your career success.

Social media can be a strong differentiator in a competitive market when the information you share is targeted, relevant, and timely. Helping your readers' advance their skill sets and improve their bottom lines will enable you to become and remain their "go-to resource" for strong relationships that result in profitability.

If you are like most professionals today, you visit the websites and social media platforms that offer the information of vendors seeking to do business with you.

Odds are that prospective buyers of your products and services perform the same kinds of due diligence. Don't fall behind your competition on this front!

Your digital footprint is critical today! So, be certain that the appropriate people in your company are busy making positive electronic impressions and guarding your corporate reputation with insight.

Social media can easily be your light at the end of the tunnel and *not* a train—unless you ignore it. In that case, it very easily *could be* a train in the form of your competitor whose digital footprint overshadows yours!

Chapter 9

MASTERING PRICE DIFFERENTIATION!

Have you ever noticed that The Rolls Royce Motor Car Company never offers you $10,000 cash back when you buy a new Rolls Royce? Or a zero-interest loan? They have no interest in presenting a low budget, cost-saving image. To the contrary, they want you to know that they only make a modest number of their fine motor cars per year, and that if you want one you had better get your deposit in as soon as possible to get on the list! This exclusivity factor justifies the price of these unique automobiles in the minds of the consumer.

How we go to market is critical in terms of the messages we send to our targeted buyers. These discussion points on differentiation have been about the choices we must make in order for what we offer to be unique when compared to our competitors. We must either creatively structure our offering in such a way that our price becomes secondary in our negotiations, based upon our customers' perception of value, or choose a way to project that we are the lowest priced, best bargain out there! I recommend the former option, not the latter. *If you gain business on price, you can lose it on price.* Anybody can give their stuff away!

So, the question becomes: How we can craft a value proposition that is more compelling than those of our competitors? And, it can get tricky here, because we need to go to market with a strong, broad-based appeal to our targeted clientele/prospects while at the same time maintaining the capability of revealing specific "value points" to individual prospects whose major buying motives have been identified.

At U. S. Learning, we define the *Value Proposition* as the perceived value and benefits imbedded within an organization's deliverables in the context of the investment required for their acquisition. Here are six ideas to keep in mind regarding possible approaches:

1. Keep the conversation with prospective buyers oriented around benefits to them, not always on financial or numerical discussions.

2. Focus on your best quality points to demonstrate that the ultimate cost over time will be less than the apparent price today, especially when compared to your competition.

3. Offer more convenience and greater accessibility than your competition does to keep your customers constantly impressed with how connected you and your company are when they need you most.

4. When talking benefits, accentuate the value points you captured from them regarding their priorities and preferences when you performed your needs analysis.

5. Constantly educate them and their people about effective usage, creative applications,

and maximum benefits of the products and services you offer.

6. Get on their side of the table and problem-solve with dedication and expertise, considering things from their point of view. Maximum collaboration pays off "big-time" in the present and will pave the way for long-term relationships.

Listen carefully to your customers' comments and use these *"price + performance"* tools to differentiate your unique value proposition. This will ensure they concur your price is fair and justified.

DIFFERENTIATING YOURSELF AND ALL YOU OFFER

- The idea behind differentiation is to go to market with a compelling uniqueness which enables you to gain market share.

- As you stand out from the crowd and provide solid, unique solutions you can move toward "Trusted Advisor" status.

- Tap the "collective intellect" of your team members to create technology, social media, and product differentiators.

- Marketing differentiation is key. Vow to outsell your competition by being an aggressive student of the latest and best practices for sales excellence.

- Remember, when your customers and prospects are "commoditizing", you need to be busy "differentiating"! Become a category of *one*.

- Experiential differentiation is making your customers say "Wow", or "Do you mean you can do that for us?!" Give them great service experiences with a personal touch and you may have them for years.

I recommend you
view this video clip:

"Differentiation"

https://vimeo.com/268188905

PART II

THE BEST VERSION OF YOU

PREMISE

Have you ever done business with someone who had such a compelling personality, manner, and code of excellence that you couldn't wait until your next encounter with them? Part II of this book will provide you with tips for fine-tuning yourself, your approach, and your actions to secure the best response. The skills and ideas covered will enable you to find and repeatedly present the best version of you to the people in your marketplace.

Chapter 10

NEVER STOP LEARNING: NEVER!

A well-informed communicator gains the interest and intrigue of others readily. People are similarly impressed with those who have an above average vocabulary.

When you set out to master the "mind game", remember that those with the sharpest *minds* generally win! Professionals learn their most critical skills by studying on their own outside of the formal training setting, and they maintain a lifetime hunger for knowledge. They also keep a dynamic spirit, positive expectations, and a determination to grow and prosper!

Since none of us can use skills, strategies, or tactics we don't know, we should dedicate ourselves to *learning*. Whether it is selling skills, management tactics, or negotiation techniques, new ideas and concepts are emerging all the time. Vow to stay on the leading edge—*not the trailing edge*—to beat your competition!

What is your perception of your own self-education and skill-building efforts in the past three years? Are you relying on past skills learned, or are you continuing to read and learn the latest and best practices that work most effectively in your marketplace today? My colleague Jim Pancero and I had a conversation recently about clients who say, *"We don't need any training at this time. We have a very experienced group of professionals selling for us."* It begs a frightening question: does *experienced* equal *trained*? Not necessarily.

Are you satisfied with where you are in your career and success path? Are you constantly at the top of your team's and your industry's performance rankings? Or do you sometimes feel you are falling behind? Do you marvel at how some of your team members and competitors snatch victory from the jaws of defeat? If your production is lagging, do you wonder what you can possibly do to make your *next* steps the *best* steps in turning things around? And, do you really have the will and determination to do the heavy lifting required to be the sales champion and competitor you see yourself as being? How do your skills stack up when compared to others in your business?

Those are a lot of questions. Here is where some of the answers lie:

1. Review where you are now compared to where you ranked 1, 5, and 10 years ago.

2. Identify the amount and nature of recent changes (positive or negative) that have occurred.

3. Identify the reasons for this change.

4. Identify what you need to do differently to improve more rapidly.

5. Decide how you need to alter your mindset about learning.

6. Identify where you want to be in one year and create an action plan.

7. Identify what goals and targets are required to achieve these numbers.

8. Identify what learning opportunities your company has

scheduled and prepare to eagerly participate.

9. Identify supplemental educational resources available and be proactive in taking advantage of those that fit.

If it was easy to be a super-star, everyone would be one! We often have to make the difficult decision: Do you want to experience the pain of discipline to learn and grow, or experience the pain of regret? Your response to the nine items listed above will provide you with a detailed, clear "snapshot" of where you are now and where you want to be. Find the extra-effort opportunities you need to consider in order for you to compete effectively and win long-term!

So, never stop learning! Get excited about what you know. Share your enthusiasm with your peers. Get everybody pumped and recount your success stories that resulted from the training you received in formal settings or on your own. Always continue to make your mind-set and your skillsets the powerful assets to propel you to the levels of excellence you have chosen for yourself!

Chapter 11

TRACKING TRENDS GIVES YOU THE EDGE!

When we are leaving the house each morning, we all need to have a feeling of confidence that we are ready for the challenges of the day. One key is to be current on our perspective of today's marketplace and the values of those we will deal with.

The effective tracking of trends should be a goal for each of us. Let's carefully evaluate current trends and how they are affecting us and our industry. When we do it well, we will be in a position to capitalize on a trend rather than become a victim of it!

According to Daniel Burrus, noted author of the best-seller, *The Anticipatory Organization*, there are two primary types of trends. There are *hard trends*—the ones that have been proven and validated—and *soft trends,* which we have observed as emerging, but have not yet been validated. When we take a close look at both, we can better deal with today's realities, and go to market with more confidence and relevance than ever.

Here are four concepts to consider in our quest to always remain equipped to face the challenges of the day:

1. Have you made a sound assessment of your approach to success in today's market? How many of us are still using "old-school ideas" that aren't working as well as they used to? Some top of mind examples include:

   a. Too much talking;

   b. Not enough listening;

   c. Shallow efforts to learn customer needs;

   d. Asking for business before we have earned the right;

   Let's make every attempt to attend the "new school" for communicating, persuading, and displaying exceptional interpersonal skills. This school entails reading the books, blogs, and articles on the latest and best practices, especially as related to each customer's specific needs and wants. Example: There is a good chance you are dealing with more *Millennials* now than *Boomers*, which means you'd better be a willing and proficient *texter*, and up to speed on the values of both age groups.

2. Listening to your marketplace is critical today. What are your customers telling you matters most to them and how does that vary from other comments? What are the circumstances that changed the dynamic? What types of solutions in your space are gaining the most traction today? Where will your best opportunities lie in the immediate future? What are the most meaningful innovations that have taken place in your industry lately, and how

do you and your company stack up in capitalizing on them?

3. One solid trend impacting all of us is the use of social media in communications. How much more engaged are you today in social media than you were one year ago? Be certain that you are communicating with each of your customers based on their preferences, (not your old habits) for best results!

4. What are you doing to assure maximum engagement with the right people in your market? Are you participating in networking events, community-related groups that will expand your sphere of influence, and conferences for learning the latest and best ideas in your field?

All of these can help. As we develop more relational capital, we can enjoy greater levels of success.

Another trend that is rapidly gaining heightened awareness is artificial intelligence. Research how it will likely affect your industry or profession. While it isn't a substitute for human intelligence or our ability to reason, it will nevertheless have a powerful impact on all of us.

Getting smarter, faster than our competition, is a prerequisite to our remaining assured of always having an edge that can make a big difference in our professional destiny!

I have surmised that the majority of people reading this book are interested in sales and marketing. Watch the video below for my "old school" vs. "new school" sales vocabulary.

 I recommend you
view this video clip:

"Old School vs. New School Selling"

https://vimeo.com/329164659

Chapter 12

MOTIVATION MAKES THE DIFFERENCE!

A motivated individual is one who has a strong, undeniable desire to achieve. This desire can be self-inspired, or it can be initiated by another source. Either way, motives are key elements in the process of achieving on-going success. It is nearly impossible to motivate someone who refuses to be motivated. Hopefully you will spot these individuals early in your interviewing process. By reviewing their track record and behavioral attributes, you will be able to make a high quality decision.

Those who have specific goals, a positive attitude, and a "can-do" spirit tend to be more receptive when it comes to being motivated. The best way managers can motivate their staff members is to create an encouraging environment around them that is consistent with desired outcomes.

The best definition of motivation I've ever seen is from Henry David Thoreau who said "Motivation is the pull of anticipation and the push of discipline." Anticipation includes our goals, objectives, dreams, and visions, and the discipline is derived from a strong work ethic and a hunger to excel.

There are two dimensions of motivation: direction and intensity. Direction is being focused on saying and doing the most productive and appropriate thing. Intensity is the amount of effort one puts into the undertaking. This gives us four variables: positive direction and low intensity (ramp up the effort!); positive direction and high intensity (Bravo!); negative direction and high intensity (Beware!); and negative direction and low intensity (Nothing much happening here!).

Now that we have covered the definitions and the structure of motivation, let's talk about practical applications. People need to go below surface thoughts and think deeply and specifically about what they want in conjunction with the why, when, and how to actually make it happen.

The answers to the 5 excellent questions (below) can go a long way toward determining each person's level of self-motivation:

1. *Do you have specific goals in writing?* When you do, the process of seeking the goal becomes more realistic. If something is important, work from a document, not just thought!

2. *Who is in the loop?* In other words, who will the key players be in the scenario of you reaching the goal or responding to your motive? What role will they play and how can you most successfully position yourself with them for the process to work?

3. *What is the next step?* You have motivated yourself to initiate the quest for what you want. Now that you are into it, frequently ask yourself, "What is the next logical step?" As you continually ask that question

and take action, you will be on track to making progress. Get others in the loop to assist in the process as needed.

4. *Are you focused on the prize and intense in your actions?* The highest achievers tend to be those who have demonstrated that they have their *afterburner for action* turned on, and they enjoy compressing more achievement into a given measurable time frame than others.

5. *Are you giving yourself deadlines for certain component parts of your vision?* Make your deadlines challenging, but realistic, to help you give your best effort.

Motivation plays a key role in the achievement we all want. This is primarily due to the multiplicative effect on how much effort is expended. The stronger the motivation (intensity), the greater the achievement and the shorter the time frame for achieving success.

One question frequently asked by leaders is, "How can I motivate my people?" One thing you can do is to make your team members feel committed to you. One great way to do that is to frequently mention your visions and those of your organization in ways that make them feel a part of a bigger picture.

Another way is to keep the following equation in mind: $P = (K + S + A) \times M$.

Legend: P is Performance

K is Knowledge

S is Skills

A is Attitude

M is Motivation

Good luck with achieving more by being more motivated!

Chapter 13

CREATING VISIONS AND GOALS FOR SUCCESS

We all know that higher achievers stand out from the crowd. Those higher achievers invariably visualize great success!

Goal-setters who have a clarified vision of desired outcomes, strong faith in their ability to achieve them, and a willingness to plan and take action, will enjoy resounding success! Uncompromised determination coupled with intense focus and follow through will enable the goal to become reality. When you determine that you are going to make your vision come about, nothing in the above list of descriptors can be short-circuited.

Just as a moving magnifying glass over an old newspaper outside on a hot, clear summer day will *never* cause a fire, the person who is not convicted to his goals

STANDING OUT FROM THE CROWD will most assuredly *falter*. Conversely, the moment you hold the magnifying glass still under a hot sun and focus the energy of the sunlight, you will see the newspaper darken and momentarily catch fire. Likewise, committed achievers who maintain their focus, never give thought to surrendering their goals, and persist regardless of obstacles, will enjoy a level of success never known by the multitudes.

Here are a few proven strategies for attaining your desired results:

TARGET (Establish) eight goal categories. The most preferred, common, ones are: Physical, Spiritual, Financial, Community, Career, Educational, Family, and Recreational. Change or choose ones that work best for you.

- Use the spoke and wheel method of charting your goals with ten hash marks on each spoke...

- The recommended process is to chart your "current reality" in each category by putting an "X" on the number that represents where you are now. After careful thought, put a bold dot on

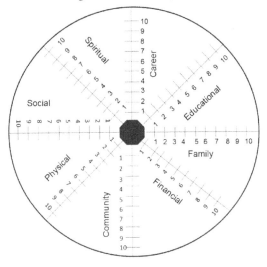

the number you want to be by the end of the year (or quarter, etc.). The deviation between the two numbers creates a constructive tension that will help energize you to action! In addition to charting the numbers, you need to create a brief narrative for the specific goals you want to achieve in each category. The more detail the better.

- Refer to your illustration every day and think about what you need to do in each category every day, week, and month, to make progress and ultimately reach your goals.

One of my favorite quotes on goals is from Paul J. Meyer. Paul said, "Whatever you fervently desire, vividly imagine, and enthusiastically act upon must inevitably come to pass!" I sat next to Paul at a banquet in Dallas one night and found him to be as big a thinker, one-on-one, as he was in his writings. His *Success Motivation Institute* made him hundreds of millions and he was having fun giving away most of his fortune in the last ten years of his life.

What would you try if you knew you could not fail? Do not fear failure! If you will visualize your significant goals and dreams, and move toward them with energized action, you can make them happen. It has been said that we *triple* our commitment and results when we write our goals down and *quintuple* our commitment and results when we assign them a time frame.

Remember, there are no unrealistic goals, only unrealistic time frames.

Marcus Aurelius said, "Dream big dreams; only big dreams have the power to move men's souls". God gave us extraordinary abilities to think, reason, decide, and act. Don't go to your grave with your music still in you. Go make something great happen!

Chapter 14

LISTEN AND LEARN

We all are frequently exposed to ideas from others—skills from internet learning, and takeaways from traditional training. We literally have great ideas whizzing by our heads every day.

The key is to capture them. Superior listening will enhance retention and our customer relationships.

Comprehending things that are vital to us out of all that we see and hear can become a daunting task. It is important we recognize and improve the means by which we process new ideas and turn them into best practices. People who don't take learning seriously usurp their opportunity to improve themselves. Let's listen and learn for *comprehension*, not just to craft a reaction.

Below are six ideas on how to get the most out of a learning opportunity. When you do these things, you will not only learn more, but profit more, from the content.

Here are the To Do's…

1. Minimize distractions and vow to have a high level of concentration as you read or listen to new ideas and key conversations, and fewer gems of wisdom will whiz past your head!

2. Develop the habit of rapid evaluation of an idea; if it is valuable to you, capture it! Write it in your journal! Say it out loud! Share it with someone on your team!

3. Recognize it as a valuable idea you will want to reference in the future and highlight the entry in a certain color for that category. If it is an actionable idea you want to move on right away, highlight it in a different color. If the input is from other than a book, write it immediately in your journal, or create a computer file for "Action Items".

4. Internalize the idea by thinking of how you will use it.

5. Energize yourself to implement the idea or skill at the next appropriate time. Some people *watch* things happen and some people *make* things happen!

6. Actualize your desired outcome by making the idea or skill work for you. Adapt it as necessary to deploy it in the framework of your success plan.

With a solid means of processing valuable ideas as you are exposed to them, you can take action and assure yourself growth and progress. Remember, it's not *what* we know, it's *what we do* with what we know that propels us to the next level.

My favorite writer in the self-help/ success space is Orison Swett Marden. In his book, *Round Pegs in Square Holes*, he wrote the following:

It is pitiable to see bright people remaining for years in occupations against which every nerve and fiber in them protests, when a change into their niche would make a new world for them!

Let's not be among those who have put learning on the back burner and continue to do today that which they did yesterday. The knowledge mass of the human race is now advancing at an amazing pace, so let's be part of the crowd that listens to comprehend, learns to capture solid ideas, and takes action to produce results!

Those who listen marginally because they are busy trying to figure out what they are going to say next are afflicted by the *whiz-by* phenomena referred to earlier. To experience a quality learning process, think comprehension and you will be able to capitalize on some great options for progress.

Capture and internalize the skills. Find your niche. Propel yourself into action and make your life a masterpiece!

Chapter 15

THE ATTITUDE
OF A WINNER

You don't often see winners *whining*—or, whiners *winning!*

The two concepts just don't go together. People with a positive attitude have chosen the 'glass is half full' philosophy rather than 'half empty', and they enjoy a better life with their positive focus and their resulting belief in self.

At U. S. Learning, we define attitude as *the spirit or demeanor one chooses to adopt and display from a given stimulus.* I'm convinced that the most important word in that definition is *"chooses"*. We all choose our attitude many times a day as various stimuli come at us, often at an unmerciful rate. Attitude is your choice, and it is a major determinant of what happens next! Optimists see the *opportunity* in every problem and the pessimists see the *problem* in every opportunity.

Those displaying a healthy positive attitude can be totally in touch with reality and still feel good about things. Determined optimists eat problems for breakfast, lunch, and dinner. Their positive spirit and *"can-do"* attitude keep them going through any adversity that stands between them and the life of achievement they have chosen for themselves.

Noted philosopher, William James said "One cannot directly choose his circumstances, but he can choose his thoughts and indirectly, yet surely, shape his circumstances". Ideally, we will always choose our thoughts and shape our circumstances with positive responses during a typical day of pursuing our dreams. If we take the high road with noble thoughts and a win-win spirit in all of our relationships, we will get better results. Don't succumb to the temptation of going negative! Don't let anything drag you down or make you unhappy! Remember, as Dale Carnegie said, "Happiness doesn't depend on any external conditions; it is governed by our mental attitude."

The failure of millions has been the outgrowth of negative expectations and the absence of the confidence and optimism we need for the victories that will take us to the next level!

A positive "winners" attitude will offer you many gateways to success that constantly elude the "whiners". Here are a few:

1. If you have an attitude that is receptive to the self-improvement process, you will enjoy learning new skills;

2. If you have an attitude that lends to serving and helping others, you will create tremendously valuable relational capital;

3. If you have an open-minded attitude about new ideas, you will have more opportunities coming your way;

4. When you display a positive attitude, you will have a more resilient demeanor which will compel people to seek you out;

5. When we have a positive attitude, we have less of a tendency to negatively pre-judge outcomes;

6. Positive thinkers get more positive results! (That's the hallmark belief of Dr. Norman Vincent Peale in his great work *The Power of Positive Thinking*)

One's attitude is often the difference between success and failure, so don't let the negatives creep into your brain and take over. You are in charge of you! You do indeed choose your attitude, so take that responsibility seriously.

Don't ever doubt the power of The Self-Fulfilling Prophecy; *"Whether you think you are going to fail or succeed, you are right!"* Muster the mental discipline to turn your stresses into strength and your problems into opportunities. When you develop the habit of doing so, you will have mastered the most critical choice you make many times a day—to constantly maintain the *attitude of a winner*!

Part II – INSIGHTS

THE BEST VERSION OF YOU

- School is never out for the pro! As you continue to learn you will cast away outmoded beliefs and skills in favor of newer, better practices. Keep learning to stand out from the masses.

- A company's team is only as good as the collective skills and talents of the team members. And that includes maintaining a positive team spirit and an eagerness to do your best, whatever your position.

- When one stops setting goals and making measurable career progress, complacency sets in and it becomes nearly impossible to progress.

- If one sets goals in writing, one will triple the commitment to the goal and the probability of achieving it.

- One's attitude of mind is a critical part of their success process. We can only be a valuable resource to our clients and co-workers if we have a positive spirit and well-thought-out positive intentions.

- "The Mind Game" is the foundation upon which all of our skills and talents rest. Without perseverance, optimism, courage, discipline, and determination, we will never achieve great things.

I recommend you
view this video clip:

"Goal Setting"

https://vimeo.com/338095055

PART III

YOUR INTERPERSONAL SKILLS

PREMISE

Good interpersonal skills enable you to be conversationally adept with others. People tend to evaluate you by how you look, what you say, how you say it, what you do, and how you do it. For others to be impressed with you, you need above average skills in conversing with others. The study of how we develop these skills begins with understanding others, their behaviors, their needs, and their current area of focus. To connect successfully with others, we should talk in terms of their interests. Understanding behavioral styles sets us up for communicating successfully with others. This Part III Section of the book will cover the four types of people and how to communicate with each for best results.

Chapter 16

SELLING WITH STYLE

Have you ever been talking to someone when all of a sudden you feel as if you are conversing with a weirdo? Southern comedian, Brother Dave Gardner, used to say, "Everybody is weird once you get to know them!"

People are different for sure, and, many have argued that the key to success in life is in understanding the categories into which each of them falls—and knowing how to tailor your approach when communicating with them.

My long-time friend and colleague, Dr. Tony Alessandra, Scott Zimmerman, and I wrote a book with the same title as this chapter. The goal of our collaboration was to address the differences in people and the varying approaches to selling different people in different ways. The concept of using behavioral styles to identify a person's attributes is quite helpful in understanding others and how they prefer to communicate.

More importantly, in this section of *Standing Out From The Crowd*, you will learn how people in different behavioral categories make buying decisions. Much research has been done to establish models of the four primary styles and how to communicate with them for best results. Since our goal is to always be the recognized leader in our competitive marketplace, our efforts to treat people as they like to be treated will give us a distinct edge.

The three dimensions of human behavior are *Assertiveness*, *Responsiveness*, and *Adaptability*. Let's look at the first two here:

1. Assertiveness is one's "Discussion Approach". On a horizontal continuum, more assertive people are on the right and less assertive people are on the left. Assertiveness is defined as the amount of effort one puts forth to influence others.

More assertive people come on stronger, speak with voice emphasis, and tend to press for decisions. Less assertive people are more laid back, speak in a consistent tone, and are in no hurry to make a decision.

2. Responsiveness reflects one's display of emotion. On a vertical continuum, less responsive people are on the top and more responsive people are on the bottom. Responsiveness is defined as the degree to which a person displays emotions through gestures, voice inflection, and non-verbal communications.

Less responsive individuals have a low display of emotion, often showing a "poker face" with few gestures. The more responsive types tend to show lots of gestures, facial expressions, and more vocal variety.

Your awareness of these two dimensions will help you create a model for understanding the types and attributes of people.

In an effort to establish a logical way to chart these two behaviors, the framework "grid" looks like this:

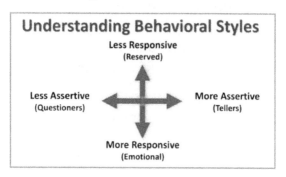

When you enclose the framework into a square, four quadrants are established which quantify the various behaviors described and reveal four different behavioral styles. They are *Drivers, Expressives, Analyticals*, and *Amiables* as shown here:

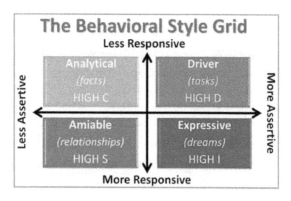

Let's discuss each "style" to understand them better.

1. Drivers are upper right on the grid, and they are a combination of more assertive and less responsive behavior. They tend to have a short attention span and are task oriented.

2. Expressives are lower right on the grid and they are a combination of more assertive and more responsive behavior. They enthusiastically try to influence others to help make their dreams and visions happen.

3. The Analyticals are upper left on the grid and are a combination of less assertive and less responsive behavior (opposite of the Expressives). They tend to be introverted, have a long-attention span, and need facts before responding.

4. The Amiables are lower left on the grid and are a combination of less assertive and more responsive behavior (opposite of the Drivers). They tend to

be warm, friendly, and relationship oriented.

Everyone is somewhere on this grid in terms of their "usual behavior" and there is no best quadrant to be in. Measurements of assertiveness and responsiveness are quantitative but not qualitative, so everyone's location on the grid is "ok". Simultaneously we should recognize that nobody is perfect. We all have both strengths and weaknesses.

The dimension we refer to as Adaptability is covered in the next chapter. My goal is to give you strategies for communicating with different people and opening up new vistas of interpersonal understanding.

Chapter 17

FINDING YOUR SUCCESS PATH WITH EXCEPTIONAL ADAPTABILITY SKILLS

Sometimes we need to step out of our "Comfort Zone" to make progress with others. If it is true that the knowledge mass is now doubling approximately every four years, we will see more ambiguity and new options than ever before as the future unfolds. The question is: how willing are we to consider new ideas and reach out to others with a different point of view in a manner that works well?

As shown above, there are four behavioral styles and your usual behavior is reflected in one of them. Whatever your style might be, it is important to learn how to communicate effectively with people

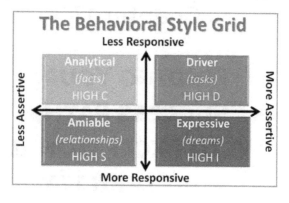

you identify as belonging to one of the other three styles. And, you must express yourself in a manner that is engaging and comfortable for them. Since there is no guarantee *they* will adapt, your best strategic approach dictates that *you* should just go ahead and do the adapting!

Dr. David Merrill offered a comprehensive definition of adaptability: "*an effort to please more people while keeping your own objectives intact; being resourceful in adapting your methods to be acceptable and understood; balanced concern for self, task and others with a willingness to step out of your own comfort zone.*"

It is a safe bet that, when you were three or four years old, your parents taught you the "Golden Rule". It is a great rule! How can you go wrong when you

"Do unto others as you would have them do unto you"? But there is another sound rule called the "Platinum Rule". I present it for your consideration—not instead of the Golden Rule, but in addition to it! The Platinum Rule is: *"Do unto others as they like to be done unto"!*

The following behavioral guidelines offer you clues as to how to adapt to others:

- DRIVERS are fast-paced, bottom line-oriented
- EXPRESSIVES are fast-paced, people-oriented
- AMIABLES are slow-paced, people-oriented
- ANALYTICALS are slow-paced, fact-oriented

Assuming you know which of the four quadrants of the behavioral style grid you are in, it is a sound recommendation that you learn the needs of those in the other three styles since about 75 percent of your communications efforts will be with people unlike you.

In order to make adaptability skills work, there are two key factors involved. First, there is the *willingness to adapt*

STANDING OUT FROM THE CROWD (which is attitudinal). You have to decide if you are willing to put forth the effort to adapt to that person in a given scenario. The second element, *the skill to adapt,* requires know-how (aptitudinal).

There are four "Strategy Keys" for adapting your communications style with others in a manner that will work well for them:

- With DRIVERS be Efficient
- With EXPRESSIVES be Stimulating
- With AMIABLES be Agreeable
- With ANALYTICALS be Accurate

These recommendations are vital for you to successfully gain and keep the attention of those in other quadrants. Whenever you utilize these keys appropriately in discussions with others, you will increase the likelihood of getting *your* desired outcome—in a shorter period. Your mastery of the strategy keys will enhance your position as a highly effective communicator.

In short, this means to sell them as they like to be sold to or manage them the way they like to be managed, we need to adapt.

To facilitate your effectiveness in adaptability, consider these four simple elements:

- What is the other person's style?

- What is yours?

- If your style differences are complementing each other and you are making good progress, keep going!

- If your style differences are getting in the way, ask yourself, "How can I adapt?"

Finding your success path through proper application of adaptability skills can give you the edge you need in a highly competitive environment.

I recommend you view this video clip:

"Adaptability Skills"

https://vimeo.com/268729107

Chapter 18

CAN YOU ID THE "STYLE" OF OTHERS WITH CERTAINTY?

The idiosyncrasies and strategies we learned about Behavioral Styles and the importance of communicating with different people differently are effective only to the degree that we can identify which of the four Behavioral Styles another person is.

Remember that, when it comes to *style*, we are dealing with a "soft science"—which means that it is inexact and imperfect. But we can still work from valid guidelines which are immensely helpful in observing and identifying the predominate style of others.

In identifying one's style there is a process which has been found to work well. And, yes, you can identify the style

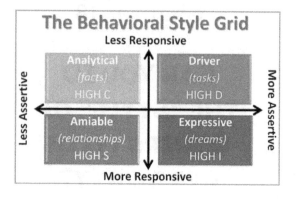

of another person with relative certainty if you practice, drill, and perfect this process over time. Like so many things, if we don't start using the ideas right away, they fade away quickly.

Human behavior is what we see and hear people say and do—their *style*. Let's start with six key components you can use in the process of developing enhanced skills for determining whether a person is a *Driver, Expressive, Analytical,* or *Amiable*:

1. Evaluate one's tendency to:

    a. Control versus Emote. That is their *Responsiveness* factor which is their propensity to show emotions and share feelings, thoughts, and opinions.

b. Ask versus Tell. This is their *Assertiveness* factor which is their discussion approach or the measure of one's pace.

c. Evaluation of these two dimensions will give you clues about their grid placement and thus their style.

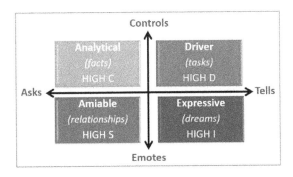

2. Observe their behavior over time. Don't rush to judgment— you may catch them in another quadrant since we all move around the grid from time to time. Just remember that there is a place we each call "home" on the Behavioral Style grid which represents our *usual behavior.* That's what we want to identify.

3. Don't make occupational assumptions. It's too easy to make a mistake. Some would think, for example, that all CPAs are Analyticals, but they are not. My CPA is a Driver. All salespeople are not Expressives, though we might assume that their extroversion would indicate that as the quadrant for salespeople. Not necessarily. Try not to stereotype since there would be obvious exceptions to what we think.

4. Don't react into Like or Dislike. That is counterproductive. Maintain your objectivity. Whether you like them or not is not the most important criterion in seeking your desired outcomes.

5. Moderate Stress clarifies Style. When we are under stress, we tend to display behavior that is more like we already are. As this exponential transition takes place, people become easier to identify by Style. A person you think is probably an Amiable,

when under stress you will note their behavior is kinder and more conforming as a result of their low tolerance for confrontation.

6. Decide their Style and verify over time. It is recommended that you practice the elements of the Style ID process often. Yes, frequent practice *will* improve your skill! As you observe people over time you will either validate your previous opinion of their style or change your mind based on other behavioral clues.

I recommend that you learn to reflexively use the six components listed above with everyone you meet in a business environment, especially customers and prospects. It will enable you to get on target and in synch with these people more efficiently and win them over interpersonally.

As you reinforce this skill, you will be on the path to not only repeatedly getting your desired outcomes, but also *standing out from the crowd!*

Chapter 19

ARE YOU PUTTING YOUR INTERPERSONAL KNOWLEDGE TO WORK?

Now that you have been introduced to several aspects of the behavioral style concept, the next step is to consider the essential points of how it all works.

First, it is important that you are relatively sure of where you are on the Behavioral Grid. This predicts how *your* behavioral style will impact others. The chart shown on the next page will give you some solid hints of where you are and where others fall on the grid as well.

We all have both strengths and weaknesses; we will call them "Building Blocks" and "Stumbling Blocks".

Survey this information and think of the various traits in terms of yourself and others with whom you communicate.

We Are Perceived By Others...		
	At Our Best	**At Our Worst**
DRIVER	DETERMINED EFFICIENT DECISIVE PRACTICAL	PUSHY HARSH DOMINATING UNSENTIMENTAL
EXPRESSIVE	AMBITIOUS STIMULATING ENTHUSIASTIC DRAMATIC	EXCITABLE UNDISCIPLINED EGOTISTICAL OVER POWERING
AMIABLE	SUPPORTIVE DEPENDABLE AGREEABLE WILLING	CONFORMING DEPENDENT WISHY-WASHY SUBMISSIVE
ANALYTICAL	SERIOUS INDUSTRIOUS PERSISTENT EXACTING	STUFFY CRITICAL INDECISIVE PICKY

ANY STRENGTH TAKEN TO AN EXTREME CAN BECOME A LIABILITY

This chart can be used for style identification, self-awareness, and strategy-building, or to simply reinforce your general knowledge of the four behavioral styles.

When you put this all together, it becomes apparent as to how you should respond to others in order to get your desired outcomes. Remember that treating people the way *they* like to be treated results in shorter sales cycles and better relationships. This is where your adaptability really comes into play.

The chart on the next page is all about the "Needs of the Four Styles". As we continue to use and internalize this information, we get better and better over time. Treating different people differently—based on their behavioral style—will net you better results with others.

When conversing with those with whom you want to do business, there are three things you should do: *Get* their attention, *Keep* their attention, and *Earn* their commitment.

In explaining the "Needs of Styles" chart notice the length of the timelines on the bar graph.

Since *Drivers* have the shortest attention span, their bar is shortest. With Drivers, *get* their attention by focusing on conclusions and actions; *keep* their attention by being efficient; and *earn* their commitment by giving them options with probabilities.

With *Expressives*, note that they have the second shortest bar denoting their impulsive nature. *Get* their attention by focusing on their dreams and intuitions. *Keep* their attention by being stimulating.

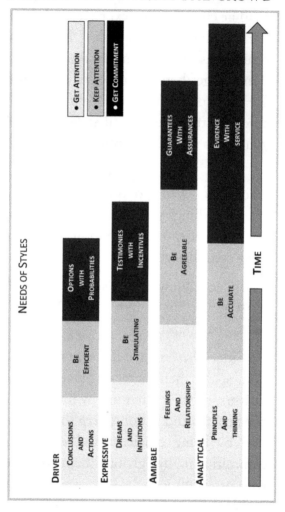

This chart shows the strategies to employ based on individual behavioral styles and the potential length of time required for a commitment to occur.

Earn their commitment by giving them testimonies with incentives.

With *Amiables,* note that their bar is longer, denoting that they need time to see how everyone else in the loop feels. *Get* their attention by focusing on feelings and relationships. *Keep* their attention by being agreeable. *Earn* their commitment by giving them guarantees with assurances.

Analyticals have the longest bar, denoting that they need time to evaluate all of the data they need. *Get* their attention by focusing on their principles and thinking process. *Keep* their attention by being accurate. *Earn* their commitment by giving them evidence with service.

This is how we sell *different* people *differently.*

Study these two charts. Capture them on your phone or print them out and learn them well! When you do, they will pay you excellent dividends!

Remember that the true sign of adaptability is to have a positive spirit with a willingness to step out of your comfort zone into the zone of another person.

When you follow these guidelines, your clients will often recognize your effort and appreciate it. This can be the difference-maker in achieving favorable outcomes.

YOUR INTERPERSONAL SKILLS (BEHAVIORAL STYLES)

- Behavioral Style is the pattern of actions others can observe and agree upon in describing one's usual behavior.

- The Assertiveness line and the Responsiveness line are the framework of the behavioral style grid. When the square is completed it reveals the Drivers, Expressives, Analyticals, and Amiables.

- Though we all wander from time to time, each person has a "home quadrant" on the grid that represents their usual behavior.

- Become a studied expert in identifying the "Style" of others. We are all in the people business and this content/skill can contribute significantly to your expertise.

- The skill of Adaptability is a critical element in succeeding with others. You need a willingness to adapt and the skill to do so.

- Be Efficient with Drivers, Stimulating with Expressives, Accurate with Analyticals, and Agreeable with Amiables.

PART IV

GAINING THE EDGE THROUGH NEGOTIATION SKILLS

PREMISE

Many think negotiating with others must be confrontational and unpleasant. That is really not the case at all. When Dr. George Lucas and I wrote *The One Minute Negotiator*, we shared with our readers the four negotiation strategies and how to successfully use them. The chapters in Part IV will give you practical skills, usable immediately, including how to deal with "Negotiaphobia", which

STANDING OUT FROM THE CROWD

most people are inflicted with, at least to a degree. If we possess the skill to pleasantly negotiate with others and reach *win-win* solutions, we will stand out from the crowd.

Chapter 20

ARE YOU PROSPERING USING NEGOTIATING STRATEGIES?

Have you ever heard of a *Mistaken Certainty*? It is when you are certain you are correct about something when in fact you are not. We all have these from time to time. These mistaken certainties need to be de-mystified. Hopefully we will have a co-worker, confidante, or family member who will set us straight before we use these untruths to miscommunicate with someone!

Similarly, there are some myths about *negotiations* that need to be de-mystified if we are going to succeed in our negotiation efforts.

Here are five such myths that you need to deal with for maximum effectiveness.

Myth #1: Negotiation is a confrontational, unpleasant process!

Fact: Not really. It certainly doesn't have to be. If we learn how to negotiate skillfully, it can be a rewarding and interesting process. We all negotiate several times a week, both personally and professionally. Seek out the best skills, learn them, and make them work for you.

Myth #2: Negotiation activities are little more than mudslinging and it's largely a waste of time and energy!

Fact: Untrue for sure. A negotiation doesn't need to be a battle. It can and should be a civilized interchange in an effort to close gaps in communication and understanding, then building a bridge for reaching a mutually acceptable agreement.

Myth #3: Since I have had little or no negotiations training, I'm sure those I negotiate with will have superior skills!

Fact: Maybe not. Remember, the disease of "Negotiaphobia" (the fear of negotiating) is rampant out there. There are far more people with marginal skills than those with advanced skills of negotiation. Just about everyone willing to do the work has the intelligence and capability to learn the tools and tactics of negotiation.

Myth #4: The best negotiators are the ones who will say or do anything to get their way. They are ruthless and untoward in their approach and you cannot rely on them to tell the truth!

Fact: To the contrary, the best negotiators who enjoy consistent successes are often people of integrity and high ethical standards.

Myth #5: The most successful negotiators are the ones who approach their opponents aggressively and relentlessly with their primary focus being on what they want!

Fact: Admittedly the toughest competitive negotiators are formidable, but most negotiation experts disagree with this myth. The best negotiators are the ones who are excellent listeners. We enable ourselves to say the right and proper next thing in a negotiation after we have learned by listening to what our customers say. That is the only way we will become aware of their true wants and needs.

When you consider the myths above and the responses to them, you will better position yourself as a true professional in the negotiation arena.

Here are three key takeaways to internalize as you advance your negotiation skills:

1. Learn the four negotiation strategies (Avoid, Accommodate, Compete, and Collaborate), and how and when to use them. Practice, drill, and rehearse until your skills are polished and reflexive.

2. When you feel a negotiation presenting itself, get your head in the game and prepare as best you can.

3. There is no substitute for planning your strategy and anticipating positions those on the other side of the table will have and confidently working through every key aspect of the negotiation process. If you treat a negotiation *casually*, you may become a *casualty*!

In order to achieve the levels of performance you desire, you really need to read at least one negotiations book a year for the balance of your career! When you do, I predict you will internalize many new skills and become more confident than ever as you strategize for success!

Chapter 21

THE SIGNIFICANCE OF THE NEGOTIATION MATRIX

The axes of our matrix contain several attributes that will enhance your understanding and usefulness of it. The vertical axis is about "Activation", with proactive on the top and reactive on the bottom. When dad steps in to calm an argument between two siblings, he usually starts with the question "Who started this?" The starter is the activator and he/she is on the top of the grid (Proactive). The other sibling would typically be the Reactive one.

The horizontal axis is about "Cooperation", with high cooperation on the right and low cooperation on the left. A mutually friendly negotiation is typically found on the right side of the matrix and the more difficult ones are on the left (less cooperative) side. This results in four quadrants (negotiation strategies) with different characteristics.

Lower left on the matrix is the AVOIDANCE strategy representing the negotiator who is less cooperative and reactive. These people have the most serious cases of *Negotiaphobia*, and they usually push back on engaging in the process.

On the lower right we have the ACCOMMODATION strategy representing those who are more cooperative and reactive. These people need to be careful not to give away the farm in their attempt to be nice and forge a relationship. We also find that not nearly as many transactions get done on the bottom half of the matrix.

The top half of the matrix (Proactive) is where there is more action! Upper left is the COMPETITIVE strategy, known to be a win-lose posture where people are fighting for the absolute best deal, even if it takes a toll on the relationship. It can get ugly fast with rigidity often personifying both sides.

The upper right-hand quadrant is the more cooperative COLLABORATIVE strategy. This is where people on both sides work to seek a win-win solution to the negotiation. If you want to be a long-term trusted advisor to the other party, it is usually worth putting the time into a collaboration, seeking a solid win-win solution with which both parties are comfortable.

Here's the major takeaway: Master your negotiation skills to demonstrate that you are confident and competent with all four strategies. Though you may have a preferred strategy, be willing and able to go to the quadrant the other party insists on occupying in order to negotiate with them successfully. For example,

I prefer collaboration, but if the person on the other side insists on competing, I can go there and hold my own without difficulty.

Once they see you can compete with them, they may be inclined to lighten up and go collaborative with you. They were trying for some low hanging fruit! As you demonstrate strength and competence with each of these four strategies, they will know that they are negotiating with a knowledgeable pro.

Since we all negotiate almost every day, it is a great skill set to possess. Learn it now and use these ideas to your advantage for the rest of your life!

I recommend you
view this video clip:

"The One Minute Negotiator"

https://vimeo.com/268100254

Chapter 22

TREATING YOUR "NEGOTIAPHOBIA"

"Negotiaphobia" is a widespread and frequently unrecognized affliction that negatively impacts people in their personal and professional lives. It is a fear of negotiating based on a desire to avoid conflict and a lack of skill. Most people have at least a light dose, and some are severely hampered by this dreaded illness. Since we all negotiate one way or another most days, we need to get treatment for negotiaphobia!

A lot of people see negotiating as an unpleasant task and avoid it when they can. Their proficiency in negotiating successfully is marginalized, resulting in low level skills. I am giving you some tools to help you become a stronger and more skilled negotiator.

Here are some tips to keep in mind:

1. As with most diseases, the first issue in *treating* negotiaphobia is admitting that you *have* it.

2. In today's business environment, many of us are charged with selling at higher profit levels than ever before. This means we need to protect margin by selling at higher prices which inevitably requires negotiation skills.

3. Be a student of negotiation skills for the balance of your career. The more skillful you become, the less fear and apprehension you will experience.

4. Our only real job security today is our own bank of relevant skill sets. Negotiation skills are near the top in payoff and results!

5. Learn and utilize the "EASY Process" for treating negotiaphobia (outlined below).

6. After you learn new skills, practice, drill, and rehearse them right away to internalize the skills so that they can be a natural reaction when you need them.

7. Keep good records of the negotiation strategies your prospects

and customers use with you. The best predictor of *future* behavior is *past* behavior. Go into each opportunity for securing a transaction with predictability and you will be better armed to succeed.

What's so EASY about negotiation? The EASY Process is a good one to learn and practice.

E is for <u>Engage</u>. In other words, get your head in the game. When you see or feel a negotiation entering the picture, be prepared and confident.

A is for <u>Assess</u>. Based on behavior observed, reputation, or past experiences, what strategy is most likely the one they will deploy? Avoid, Accommodate, Compete, or Collaborate?

S is for <u>Strategize</u>. Develop the strategy that you feel will best serve you based on your prediction of their strategy. You will better protect yourself and increase your probability of success.

Y is for <u>Your</u> approach in dealing with them.

STANDING OUT FROM THE CROWD

This is your <u>EASY</u>, one-minute drill to treat negotiaphobia and succeed more often.

Whether you personally prefer Avoidance, Accommodation, Competition, or Collaboration, learn and get comfortable with all four so that you will possess a broad number of strategies in your future negotiations.

You can't perform beyond your skill sets, so get hungry for all you can learn about negotiations and you will be a more formidable player in your market.

Chapter 23

REALLY HOT SALES NEGOTIATIONS STRATEGIES

We have all heard that "Knowledge is Power". I have never seen a more profound example of that truism than in the learning, practicing, and using of negotiation skills in our challenging marketplaces.

Another useful adage to include in our discussion is, "A Journey of 1,000 Miles Begins with the First Step." That concept applies here as well. Anyone who is suffering from Negotiaphobia (the fear of negotiating) needs to take a deep dive into learning negotiation skills. That's the first step in your journey towards dramatic improvement in sales results.

Once you learn the basics of how to overcome Negotiaphobia, you will be able to clearly see why it is important that you always continue your quest for more knowledge in the negotiation arena.

There are many great books and courses on the topic and, as you learn more, your payoff, personally and professionally will increase over time. School is never out for the professional, so eagerly approach this continuing learning opportunity and your confidence will grow and your results will soar.

We have heard that "Mindset must precede Skillsets". Vow to develop confidence in your ever-improving skills.

A great "first step" in your journey towards acquiring exceptional negotiation skills is found in the list shown on the next page. These five "Self-Talk Examples" serve as indicators as to anyone's level of negotiation confidence based upon a survey completed by themselves. Consider these and identify whether you are in the *Doubter Group* or the *Confident Group*.

Self-Talk for Doubting Negotiators:

1. In negotiating, I've always thought there has to be a winner and a loser, and I lack the confidence to think I can win.

2. Negotiating is unpleasant and confrontational, and I'm not the kind of person to participate in that.

3. I hate the thought of a tough negotiation, and I do my best to avoid any of them.

4. I know there must be some important negotiation skills, but I don't know what they are, and really don't want to know.

5. I dread this encounter, because I know she is going to beat me up on price, and I'm certain that my negotiation skills don't match hers.

Healthy Self-Talk for Confident Negotiators:

1. I've studied negotiations and am confident in the skills I have learned.

2. I can negotiate in a professional manner and protect our turf (margin) without compromising the relationship.

3. I love a good negotiation since it helps me stay sharp and confidently use my skills.

4. I am continuing to study negotiation skills and reading about various tactics which improve my results.

5. Negotiations, when done well, can be collaborative, and help me gain business while advancing relationships.

Of the two mindsets displayed in the above comments, who do you think is going to be more successful? Obviously the confident negotiator who has studied, learned the critical skills, and practices them frequently. This posture also speaks to the power of positive self-talk!

Here are eight "hot tips" for negotiation excellence (Some are explained in more depth in the following Chapters).

1. Negotiation Chips: Red, Green, or Blue (next chapter)

2. Posturing and when and how to use this skill

3. The Negotiation Matrix with four negotiation strategies

4. The "DMU"—The Decision-Making Unit

5. Differentiated Offerings—and why they are important

6. Confidence without Arrogance—how to utilize this component

7. Negotiation Strategy Adaptation—knowing when and how to employ it

8. Trusted Advisor Status—how negotiating well helps you achieve this valuable position

Our goal is to impart enough negotiation skills that you will become more intrigued with the subject and start to learn more tactics which you can implement right away.

Chapter 24

BOOST YOUR BARGAINING POWER

In this chapter, we will cover "Bargaining Chips" and the positions we want to establish early in each negotiation. From the very beginning, it is important to give the other side solid signals about the significance we attach to certain chips.

As Sun Tzu said centuries ago in his work, *The Art of War*, "Every battle is won before it's ever fought."

He was obviously playing off of the importance of planning. Effective planning is rule number one in negotiation preparation!

Bargaining Chips are defined as factors in a negotiation which often vary in importance to each of the sides at the table. You need to establish the value of each chip in advance. This enables you to qualify them in importance and designate such by descriptors (e.g. Red, Blue, or Green). Some negotiators may be prepared to make concessions on some issues of lesser importance to them while fighting vigorously for others based on the perceived value to their side.

We recommend labeling all bargaining chips using the colors Red, Blue, or Green. The chips are then defined as follows:

1. Red Chips – These are issues that are not to be violated. They may be subject to laws, regulations, company policy, or your boss's directive. If they are ever compromised, even to a minor degree, it should be only in dire situations and within acceptable guidelines to all parties affected.

2. Blue Chips – These are issues you very much want to capture. Blue chips can be the difference between an excellent outcome and one that is only fair. You want to work hard to get your Blue Chips.

3. Green Chips – These are issues that would be nice to have, but

you could give them up. As they are of lesser importance to you, keep in mind that they still have value associated with them. They could even be a Blue Chip to the person across the table. Don't just use them as a "throw away item". Hold on to them for as long as practical.

In your planning process, devote quality time to considering the value of each chip you can think of that might come into play in the upcoming negotiation. Write down the value points associated with each and the potential positive and negative outcomes when you capture them or give them up. The great negotiators have this information carefully clarified before they go into a negotiation.

Another thing the most skilled negotiators do is ask key questions. The answer to each will provide clear signals as to how much value the other side attaches to an issue. The ultimate win is when you give up a Green Chip to them but gain a Blue Chip in return! Keep in mind that different parties may have different values attached to the same chip, which is the reason you want to gain as much clarity as possible in the beginning.

Some have said that negotiating is like playing a high stakes chess game, because gaining the most desirable results is usually based on careful planning and effective strategizing.

Some examples of playing with chips can be very simple. Remember when Brer Rabbit said to Brer Fox, "You can do anything but please don't throw me in the briar patch?" He did not reveal that the briar patch was the safest place he could go. When Brer Fox threw him in, he was happy!

On the other hand, some ploys with chips can be so complicated that we don't even recognize the ramifications until after the negotiation is over!

So here are your takeaways on this negotiation topic to keep in mind:

1. Devote enough time to negotiation planning so that you go in with confidence and a have good handle on the dynamics of all the chips.

2. Anticipate various outcomes so that you can competently assess all chips and their value to your side.

3. Give substantive thought to what you think the other sides' positions will be. Past experience with them can be very helpful if available. Remember that the best predictor of *future* behavior is *past* behavior.

4. Keep your overall strategy in mind as you discuss chips. For example, you don't want to damage a long-term collaborative relationship by overplaying your attempt to get a Blue Chip. Don't do something that you might well regret later.

5. Similarly, if in a competitive negotiation, don't be reluctant to work hard to get that Blue Chip, even if you have to assert yourself to get it. Remember that competitive encounters are customarily "win-lose", and there is not much of a relationship in place anyway.

6. Keep in mind to establish value on Green Chips, even if you plan to give them up. This way you might well get more in return for it.

Plan, strategize, and anticipate responses from the other side and you will win your share of the most valuable chips!

Chapter 25

BE A POWER LISTENER

It becomes evident fairly quickly to those on the other side of the table in a negotiation or sales encounter whether you are really listening. Here's a tip to prove to them that you are. When you ask a question, listen carefully to their answer. Then ask another question on the same topic that probes deeper. They will know you are fully engaged in the conversation!

We don't tend to think of listening as a *power activity* because in and of itself, it has historically been thought of as a passive behavior rather than a proactive one. Now is the time to change that. As my good friend, Harvey Mackay, said in one of his recent articles, "None of us can learn anything when we are talking". When you are conversing with a client, prospect, superior, or even a family member, clarity of communication is critical. Being a skilled listener is not only a respectful activity, it will improve your efficiency in negotiating with others. It will also help you be more convincing and build trust that can facilitate desired outcomes.

Here are 7 tips to help you become a better negotiator by asking insightful questions and maximizing your *power listening* skills:

1. Vow to concentrate on what the other person is saying. Maintain eye contact. Take notes when appropriate and remember that first and foremost we must discipline ourselves to always listen for context and understanding.

2. Seek clarity on the topics you present to assure that effective communication is taking place. To do this, ask concise questions regarding the topics being discussed, based on what you have heard and noted. This verifies to them that you understand their position so far. Probe for detail when

appropriate and you will gain enhanced understanding.

3. Remember that open-ended questions will get you more in-depth answers than closed-ended questions. An example of an open-ended question might be: "Based upon what you have told me so far, what are the two or three top outcomes you and your company are hoping to gain?" (This is a great place to refer to the notes you have taken!).

Conversely, a closed-ended question could be: "Are you hoping to get a solution in place before the end of the month?" (This could elicit a one-word answer.)

4. Repeat key ideas you have identified from the conversation so far to confirm to your customer that clear communications are taking place. Restate some of their thoughts and conclusions so that you can take the dialog to the next level. As

you extrapolate their thoughts into an advanced understanding of what they want, your customers and prospects will be impressed with your skills and pleased with your action-oriented spirit.

5. Confirm what your resourceful responses to their ideas will be going forward. They will respect your demonstrated ability to truly understand their position. This can soften the often-difficult nature of many negotiations.

6. Perform the promised function or actions with timeliness and expertise and you will be in the minority of great negotiators. Your customers will appreciate your on-time follow up and conscientious approach. That builds trust!

7. Check back to confirm that actions agreed upon have been taken, what the results are so far, and how their expectations going forward are being

addressed, so that your next steps will be clear. Your customers will always respect and value your proactivity.

Ask great questions and engage your power listening skills, and you will enjoy more successful negotiations and greater achievement than ever before.

Chapter 26

WHY DON'T WE COMPROMISE?

My partner and co-author of *The One Minute Negotiator*, Dr. George Lucas, and I burned through dozens of legal pads brainstorming ideas and training concepts while writing the book. In fine-tuning the content, we talked a great deal about various techniques, tactics, and strategies, including the *Compromise* tactic.

We agreed that it is an often misunderstood aspect of negotiations. If I am selling a car and you drive it, then ask me how much I want and I say $8,500 and you agree, that sounds like perfection -- does it not? This is not really a negotiation or a compromise, but rather, an up-front agreement, and while it sounds good at the time, often neither party is particularly happy.

On the way home, you would likely begin to think that you paid too much and might have been able to buy the car for less. On the other side of the equation, when I go to the bank to deposit your check, I might start thinking that I could have asked more than $8,500 for the car, thus leaving money on the table. Would a compromise have been a better solution? Sometimes it will get the deal done, but often the same emotions are evoked.

An upfront agreement *sounds* like total bliss, but it is only through the process of negotiation that we can reach an agreement both sides feel is in their best interest. Almost all people over-emphasize price in negotiations, just as in the car example. A savvy negotiator will tell you if they let you set the price and you let them set the terms and deliverables, they will beat you every time.

A case in point was when George and his wife bought their home. The seller had once again reduced the price. He was convinced that the seller was at or near his base price and felt he could live with the price as is, but only if he received something of value in return. He worked with his real estate agent to make an offer that was very close to the seller's asking price, but with a fairly long list of inclusions.

George included a number of repairs, an extensive home warranty policy, and also requested three light fixtures the seller planned to take with him. The seller agreed to George's terms.

This is an example of what can happen when you focus exclusively on price versus taking time to understand the overall aspects of a deal. Since a lot of people think that compromise is the quickest path to getting a deal done (and it might be), sometimes the compromise tactic is deployed too soon. Compromise is the most used and abused tactic in negotiations. Remember, compromise is not a *strategy*—it is a *tactic*.

We define compromise as a mathematical calculation to split the difference between the positions taken by the sides in a negotiation.

In the car sale example, if I was asking $8,500 and the buyer offered $7,500, then compromise would have us add the two numbers together and then divide by two and be at $8,000. Is that really the right price? Not necessarily. How can the average of two likely wrong numbers put on the table, added together, and divided by two make everyone happy?

In reality, it makes no one happy. If the buyer really thought the car was only worth $7,500 and paid $500 more than that, he would not be happy. Likewise, I would not be content with $500 below what I was convinced was a fair price.

Compromise can play a prominent role in negotiations, but it works best with these 4 provisos:

(1) When used very late in the negotiation process;

(2) When there is a relatively small gap between the two positions;

(3) When it can be tied to an immediate agreement, and;

(4) Consider the value of your time and money – it may be worth giving up $250 to get the deal done and moving on.

There is something to be said for simply gaining closure. You don't want to kill 10,000 brain cells on a hundred-dollar deal!

Chapter 27

NEGOTIATIONS...
THREAT OR
OPPORTUNITY?

Years ago, a call came in one morning from a local CEO of a company with 80 salespeople to inquire about me addressing their annual sales meeting. In the course of the conversation, he said "As you know Don, we are a Memphis-based firm and our meeting is only 45 days out. What is the best fee you would quote us for a 1-hour keynote speech?" I'm thinking local, next month, no travel—easy deal, so I gave him my best quote in hopes of getting the assignment.

We scheduled a face-to-face meeting for two days later to further discuss the opportunity to work together. It was only then that I realized my fee quote was simply my opening bid in his eyes! He was now ready to start negotiating! I learned a lot from him. His decades of relentless negotiations overshadowed my modest skill in that arena. Years later, after becoming a student of negotiations, I realized the depth of the topic, and the unlimited opportunities to excel by learning the skills of negotiating effectively.

In this Chapter, I want to share with you some simple but helpful tips for advancing your negotiation prowess. First, accept the fact that we all negotiate just about every day, so it makes good sense to have the skills to do it well. Unfortunately, when I inquire, it turns out that a relatively small percentage of my audience members say they have read a book on negotiations or attended a seminar on the topic!

Here are some tips that will help tilt negotiations in your favor:

1. Vow to become a skilled negotiator and you will find it financially and psychologically rewarding! And that doesn't mean reading one book. Become a student of the subject.

2. Know that negotiating does not have to be confrontational.

It can be a pleasant win-win process in many cases once we learn how to use the strategies.

3. Practice the skills you learn on a daily basis; like with your dry cleaner on when he'll have your cleaning ready, or your spouse on where you are going for dinner. (A collaborative approach is definitely recommended for *that* negotiation!) By constantly exercising your negotiation skills whenever you have the opportunity, you'll become better at using them at work.

4. Learn the needs and desires of the person you are negotiating with by being a good listener. This will enable you to identify their Blue, Red, and Green "bargaining chips". (See Chapter 24.)

5. When beginning a negotiation with someone that you might want to purchase something from, ask the question, "How negotiable are you?" This implies that surely they will

negotiate. The only question then becomes how much and based upon what conditions. You will get an early feel for their position.

6. Sometimes your willingness to make a concession can soften their position and get you postured for a better deal. But, try to get something in return.

7. If you have "Negotiaphobia" (the fear of negotiating), use the recommended treatment and new skills you have learned in Chapter 22.

8. Once you have mastered the skills, you will find that there is no viable reason for you to be threatened or reluctant to negotiate.

Part IV – INSIGHTS

GAINING YOUR EDGE THROUGH NEGOTIATIONS

- In negotiating with others there is no substitute for planning. Understand their wants and needs, assess their preferred approach, and strategize accordingly.

- Do not buy into the premise that negotiating with others must be confrontational and unpleasant. To stand out from the crowd try pleasant win-win strategies (Collaboration) first.

- Learn to treat any "Negotiaphobia" you may have. Maintain a high interest and determination for improved negotiation skills. The more skillful you become, the more confidence you will have.

- Learn the four negotiation strategies and when to use each. They are Avoidance, Accommodation, Competitive (Win-Lose), and Collaborative (Win-Win).

- Keep "Negotiation Chips" in mind as you strategize (Red, Blue, and Green). Know at all times what you are giving up and what you are gaining.

- Remember that the best predictor of future behavior is past behavior. If you have past negotiation experience with them, this will give you predictability and clues as to how to succeed with them this time.

PART V

YOUR LEADERSHIP MAKES THE DIFFERENCE

PREMISE

We all have the challenge to lead from time to time. Perhaps you have a managerial position, or maybe you simply want to lead your company's sales force in annual production. Either way, if we display leadership competencies, we will progress in our chosen endeavor more rapidly. This part of the book will cover ideas that you can implement right away to create the image of a leader, and progress more efficiently toward your desired outcomes with others. There are many do's and

STANDING OUT FROM THE CROWD

don'ts in the leadership arena, and we will cover multiple issues and skills, and how you can use them for best results.

Chapter 28

IS YOUR TALENT DEVELOPMENT PROCESS CREATING WINNERS?

Strong leaders are perceived as exceptional people who deserve to stand out. A leader of marginal talent seldom impresses anyone.

Leaders are learners, and they inspire each team member to be one as well! The learning cycle is defined as the length of time that takes place between the *introduction* of a skill and the *point* at which it is internalized and effectively utilized by the team member.

Anything we can do to keep the learning cycle short will pay handsome dividends, since increasing the skills of a team member puts competence on the street sooner! In order to facilitate this goal, we need to understand and use the "Learning Development Model" which has 5 stages.

The first is the *Energized Beginner*. These are the new people you have just on-boarded who are customarily excited about their new position and are eager to learn what must be done to succeed. Keep their enthusiasm high by giving them all they need to progress in a timely manner. When they display a swift absorption rate, ramp it up a notch. If it moves too slowly, they might well lose interest.

The second stage of the model is the *Reluctant Novice*. Don't be alarmed, but it is often the case that after an introduction to stage one, some beginners experience a bit of reluctance and can start thinking that the business is more complicated than they had anticipated. What they need from you is encouragement, assistance, and advice. Let them know that this is normal and work with them to progress.

The third stage in the model is the *Tentative Performer*. Now they are starting to get it! Here's where we encourage the "Practice, Drill, and Rehearse" exercise.

The Learning/Development Model

1. Energized Beginner

2. Reluctant Novice

3. Tenative Performer

4. Component Producer

5. Internalized Professional

That will help them move more quickly to the next stage.

The fourth stage is the *Competent Producer*. For example, if they are in sales, this is the point at which they have become knowledgeable enough about your product or service to perform without constant oversight in the marketplace. They have demonstrated the capability to get it done. Stay with them as they need your counsel.

The fifth stage in the model is the *Internalized Professional*. These people are near or at the mastery level. It usually takes some time to get there, but your appropriate utilization of the Learning Development Model will increase the probability that they will become a high-level performer sooner. Their reflex actions and verbalizations are on time and on point. Their demonstrated confidence impresses their prospects and they know what to do to get results.

We have probably all had the experience of losing a sale, and when driving away we realize within two minutes what we should have said instead of what we did say that would have cemented the deal! The *Internalized Professional* has learned this lesson well and constantly guards against that happening.

Jim Kleeman and I made a number of appearances together some years ago. At one meeting in Chicago, he was proclaiming the importance of training to the audience of entrepreneurs. He was interrupted by an audience member who said *"Jim, what if I spend a lot of time and money training my people and they LEAVE?"* Jim went down into the audience right up to the man and said, *"What if you don't and they STAY!"* Everyone laughed but made notes—they got it.

The Learning Development Model offers you the proven pathway to always be fine-tuning your training and development process. When you use it as your constant guide, you will be a more *successful leader* because you will have a more *successful team*!

Chapter 29

IS YOUR TEAM-BUILDING STRATEGY WORKING?

No matter how well your team is doing, there is always room for growth and progress. None of your team members are at their intellectual limit for learning. Given the proper encouragement, they could all be putting forth more effort. Can you get your team members to reach a little higher?

One of my clients who is also a personal friend owns several car dealerships. Earlier in his career, he worked for Roger Penske (also a client), who owned close to 300 dealerships.

In his management capacity, my friend reported directly to Roger and, every December, he and Roger had a phone call to discuss projections for the coming year.

During these calls, Roger would always ask him, *"What is your goal for number of units sold next year?"* In response, my friend gave him a number, then Roger would say, *"OK, now tell me what your 'stretch goal' is"*. My friend would think a moment, then give Roger a higher number. Before the call was over, Roger would always say, *"Why don't we just go ahead and make your stretch goal your regular goal? You've got a great team and you can do it!" What do you say to that?"* I think the correct answer to that particular question was always, *"Yes sir, OK!"*

My friend told his sales group that Mr. Penske complimented him on what an outstanding team they had. Then, he shared the *stretch goal* for the team and let everyone know what their additional contribution would need to be to reach that goal. They all agreed, and they invariably hit it!

Any individual sub-standard performance resulted in a brief conference to discuss production issues and make course corrections. Sharp team-builders are always ready to talk about performance issues.

When you have solid objectives in place and you know the exact average sales results of your team members, you can accurately project the number of salespeople you will need to have in order to reach these objectives. This is how you make the numbers work.

Have you ever noticed in team-building things don't always go perfectly? Just when you think your team is totally intact, three people don't show up the next day! One's truck broke down, another's dog died, and the third had to go get his brother-in-law out of jail, and on and on ad infinitum!

When you have people on the team who lose their velocity—regardless of the reason—those people are, according to leadership guru, Dr. Warren Bennis, experiencing a *Vortex of Adversity*. As a skilled leader, one of your prime responsibilities is to keep every team member producing at a high level while giving them everything they need to grow and avoid getting caught up in such a vortex.

One of the most common mistakes leaders make is managing and leading everyone the same way. It would be easier if they could do it, but no single formula fits everybody. There is an old saying in teambuilding that you "hire 'em in *masses* – train 'em in *classes* – Kick 'em into the field on their *posteriors* – and see if their performance *passes*! (I cleaned that one up somewhat for you☺). It's not that simple anymore.

The best antidote to a disappointing attempt at mass teambuilding is developing an in-depth knowledge base of the strengths, weaknesses, needs, and priorities of each team member. You might say, *"That would take too much time; we could never afford to do that!"* Believe me, you can't afford NOT to do it! Manage each one individually while having policies and procedures to which they all adhere.

Obviously, you always want to minimize turnover and maximize individual performance. That means you must go deep to understand your people, analyze their production issues, and offer solid suggestions for correcting their specific problems. At the same time, you must instill them with the confidence in themselves required to reach their very own *stretch goals*.

Your team-building strategy will succeed in direct proportion to how well you are able to create a path to a Vortex of *Achievement* (instead of *Adversity*) for each member of your team. Once you're certain they are buying-in to the concept and prepared to do the work, turn them loose and watch them perform!

Chapter 30

DEVELOP THE ATTRIBUTES OF LEGENDARY LEADERS

The debate continues. Are strong leaders born or made? My belief is that, while some talents are inherent, impressive leadership abilities are most often displayed by those who have learned the skills and values needed to excel in today's arena. I'm convinced that these qualities are teachable and learnable, and that the six attributes discussed below have been consciously adopted by those who are inarguably recognized as legendary leaders.

Vision – The Bible tells us, "When there is no vision, the people perish!" It is incumbent upon leaders to establish and advance a solid vision for the future and to make each team member feel a part of it. Leaders are highly aware of the track records and capabilities of their team members and can, with reasonable predictability, project into the future the attainment required to make visions become reality.

Credibility – High performing leaders know that *what* is right is more important than *who* is right. They objectively require accountability throughout the organization, including in their own areas of responsibility. These gifted individuals have a reputation for honesty with all parties and are known for dealing in truths. These traits not only impress the team members but make them eager to buy-in to the leader's vision and respond with inspired actions of their own.

Competence – The quality of being competent is best described as possessing the skill and ability to achieve the goals and objectives set forth. Most leaders achieved the position they currently hold, largely by displaying abilities that impressed upon others their likelihood of getting the job done and they have exhibited an enviable track record of outstanding achievement. They are eager learners themselves and require that their people be as well. These leaders also give those they lead all of the support and positive examples needed to excel.

Trustworthiness – We all know that we cannot demand that others trust us. Trust must be earned! This can only be done when we demonstrate impeccable integrity, and genuine concern for others who share our mission. Trustworthy leaders are known for keeping promises and following through with pledges and plans. We have all learned that people who display manipulation and conniving precepts are *not* to be trusted. The polar opposites of these people are the leaders who earn trust on a daily basis by actually "walking their talk".

Humility – Humble leaders reject egotism and largely focus on others rather than on themselves. They can be confident without being arrogant. Great leaders give the credit to team members for significant achievements and take the blame for non-performance (while simultaneously striving to increase the former and eliminate the latter). Humility trumps egomaniacal behavior every time.

Innovation – Legendary leaders work hard at being at the forefront of their industry. They do their homework, investigate new opportunities, and are willing to take reasonable risks. They know that to be a market leader, innovation and creativity must be part of the formula. They track trends with diligence, make decisions wisely, and always work to be on the leading edge in their chosen spaces.

These six attributes in a leader offer a high probability of organizational success. High achievers who share these strengths are constantly fine-tuning and tweaking everything required for reaching their goals quicker and growing their team members' capabilities more proficiently.

As they improve processes and inspire their team, the inevitable result is evidenced by multiple successful outcomes as well as an even more impressive image and reputation for innovation!

With each new challenge, legendary leaders rely on the attributes they have accumulated to progress into the unknown with sound strategies, a noble vision, and concern for their team members. What a pleasure it is to be led by such a person. They definitely *stand out from the crowd!*

Chapter 31

ARE YOU CREATING POSITIVE EMPLOYEE MORALE?

My treasured friend and noted author, the late Og Mandino, who wrote *The Greatest Salesman in the World*, used to say, "Find a positive way to say it and you will have an organization of higher morale".

I concur. The era of issuing edicts and strong-arming others repeatedly is history for insightful leaders. If we want our team to thrive, innovate, and make a positive contribution to our success, we need to create and cultivate an environment that is conducive to progress and growth. It is really difficult to create positive employee morale when the mindset of the organization or sales leader is negative, coercive, or unpleasant.

The coercers need to learn that their pushiness works much like knocking on a turtle's shell to get him to stick his head out!

One of the most powerful things we can do is set a positive example. Here are 7 things you can do to make a positive difference in your organization and its morale:

1. Keep in mind the "Leadership Limitation Syndrome". It suggests that employees are very unlikely to have a better attitude or skillset than their supervisor. For best results, team leaders should set their standards high. So, demand more of *yourself* and you will be an inspiration to *your team*.

2. Handle problems with confidence and determination, and your people will be more likely to do the same, thus creating a solution-based organization. When everybody is focused on *the positive*, more momentum is created, and greater results are gained.

3. Inspire positive energy. Display your own positive energy to the

group anytime you can. We all need our batteries recharged from time to time, and you can be the source of these renewals.

4. Share wins with team members instead of claiming them strictly for yourself. Take responsibility for losses—it's one of the prices of leadership. Then, identify the positive insights that were imbedded within the loss.

5. Remember Ken Blanchard's principle from *The One Minute Manage*r, "Catch people doing something right! Recognize their achievement in front of the team when you can for best results and positive impact on your organization's morale."

6. Negative events and significant challenges justify the need for talented leaders. Every challenge or negative event generally contains the seeds of new ideas, creativity, and solutions. So, welcome any setbacks you encounter with a smile rather

than allowing crisis thinking and negativity to prevail.

7. Don't forget to enable FUN to happen in your company. If we get four to six good laughs a day, we will be more productive and encouraged to drive on.

I invite you to enjoy this writing by one of my favorite self-help experts, Elbert Hubbard

I wish to be simple, honest, natural, frank, clean in mind and clean in body, unaffected, ready to say, 'I do not know', if so, it be. To meet all people on an absolute equality – to face every obstacle and meet every difficulty unafraid and unabashed. I wish to live without hate, whim, jealousy, envy or fear. I wish others to live their lives too, up to their highest, fullest, and best. If I can help people, I will do it by giving them a chance to help themselves; and if I can uplift or inspire, let it be by example, inference, and suggestion, rather than by injunction or dictation. I desire to radiate life!

The audience for this information is not limited to management alone. Each professional at every level of your team can—and should—buy in and take the initiative to help create the positive organizational morale required for the massive success you deserve! When they do, they are on the fast track to becoming the valued leaders of tomorrow.

Chapter 32

COACHING FOR SUPERIOR PERFORMANCE

Most of us coach at one time or another. Maybe it's as a sales team leader, general manager, parent, or youth sports coach. What is coaching about anyway? This writer defines it as "Assisting your people in developing the correct attitudes, habits, and skills that enable superior performance".

In terms of attitude, you may have heard the phrase, Mindset precedes Skillset. Anyone who lacks the right attitude is trying to build on a weak foundation. Another thing critically important about attitude is the impact one's attitude has on other team members. A *positive* attitude is contagious, but so is a *negative* one!

At any given time, every team member is either a *resource* or a *burden* to the rest of the team. As a coach, your first job is to keep *all* team members on the *resource* side of the continuum. Team members that inhabit the *burden* side will slow down the rest of the team. It's not possible for a team to run smoothly if a monkey wrench is thrown into the gears!

Then, we have the all-important topic of skill-building. No one can perform beyond their skill set or their knowledge base. A winning coach is focused on training and preparation as well as coaching. All three of these factors must be present for top performance to be realized. Your job is to implant within *all* of your team's members the skills and attitudes that will take each of them—*and the team*—to legendary levels of achievement.

Here are six tips for superior performance coaching:

1. Monitor performance levels and specific skill sets so that you can address the current issues in a timely and efficient manner.

2. Use one-on-one coaching sessions to teach skill improvement;

it may be as simple as changing the wording in dealing with a customer complaint.

3. Keep in mind that training and the perfecting of reflex actions are not customarily achieved with a one-time effort; the code is: "Practice, drill, and rehearse!"

4. Role-playing is an effective method of coaching your team members for improvement. If they perfect a skill in front of their team members, they will more than likely handle it well in front of customers.

5. Raise their sights for functioning at higher levels; something like; "Megan you are doing pretty well, but with all the potential you possess, you haven't begun to reach your optimum performance level." Cause them to stretch; when they share with you what their goals are, say "That's pretty good, Brad. Now tell me what your 'stretch goal' is."

6. One of the best things you can ever do for a team member is to get them to develop a reading habit! Leaders *are* readers. Press them on how many skill-building books they plan to read this year. Individuals who discipline themselves to excel in self-education will have a better shot at rising to the top!

A bonus point on the coaching topic comes to us from legendary UCLA basketball coach John Wooden, who said, "A true performer should have character, not be a character."

I was amused when I read that when Coach John Wooden recruited Bill Walton, and told him all of the players on his team would have a short, neat haircut. What happened next? Dozens of schools had been trying to recruit the seven-foot superstar, so he said, "Coach, I'm not cutting my hair!"

Coach Wooden said "Well, we will miss you, son". Walton was at the barber shop that afternoon!

As coaches dedicated to winning, let's do all we can to enable superior performance and nurture character development for every one of our team members—without usurping discipline. This will give them a genuine opportunity to enjoy a life of high achievement!

Chapter 33

SKILLS OF MANAGING AND LEADING OTHERS

Whether you are in the hierarchy of management in your company or you aspire to be, there are basic and advanced skills that, when utilized effectively, can be the determining factor in achieving superior results. All managers are challenged to lead their teams for effectiveness and improved organizational success.

Let's focus on the difference between *Management* and *Leadership*, and some of the critical skills that can help you propel both your performance and that of those you lead. As you get better at what you do, those who follow your lead will improve from the example you set!

The goal of Part V is to assist you in sorting out the most important skillsets for long-term success as a leader. Here are some definitions from my years of experience in teaching and developing these skills.

1. Leadership Defined – The art of using persuasive skills and the power of position to influence the attitudes and behaviors of others toward exceptional performance. Leadership Style is the spirit with which you do it. *We* need to be the kind of person they are eager to follow.

2. Management Defined – Here's Dr. Peter Drucker's take on it: "Management is about *tasks*; Management is a discipline, but it is also about your team; every management success or failure is about the success or failure of a manager; the vision, dedication and integrity of managers determine whether there is *management* or *mismanagement*."

3. Defining Differences Between the Two – Leadership is largely about *people*, and management is largely about *tasks*. Good *managers* get the job done

through others; Good *leaders* achieve their goals while simultaneously inspiring their team members to be high achievers as well.

4. Emerging Trends – We have reached the point where issuing edicts and making demands as standard operating procedure are outmoded – only to be used by exception. We each need to be the kind of leader that is a pleasure to follow champion of change and to get the best from our team.

5. Purpose – When you espouse a magnetic, compelling purpose, your people will follow you just about anywhere. Strong leaders get people both energized by their vision and eager to embrace it.

6. The Issue of Trust – Your people want to work for a BOSS who they know, like, and trust!

7. Top Performers – Those at the head of a company or department – need to be *confident*

and *competent*. To be a top performing leader or manager, respect your subordinates, treat them equitably, honor their dignity, train and educate them appropriately, and let them know that you expect great things from them.

8. Education – Let each of your people know that you subscribe to the principle of eagerly seeking self-education. As they see you learn and grow, they will be more inclined to learn and grow themselves.

These tips are designed to help you be the best in your efforts to lead and manage people. As you encourage them to improve and achieve, display that you are also reaching out to grab the rest of your destiny! You will be an inspiration for those on your team to do the same.

Chapter 34

THE POWER OF A POSITIVE TEAM SPIRIT

It has been my pleasure through the years to do some speaking and training for the ServiceMaster Corporation. Years ago, I met its Chairman, William Pollard, who wrote a great book entitled *The Soul of The Firm*. In it he said, "People want to work for a cause, not just a living. When there is alignment between the cause of the company and the cause of its people, move over, because there *will be* extraordinary performance!"

If you didn't show up for work, how long would it be before someone missed you? Are you a positive force for good? At any given time, each team member is either part of the problem or part of the solution. Strive to be a constant *resource!* No one really wants to be referred to as "high maintenance" or a "drama queen".

STANDING OUT FROM THE CROWD

The best way to be a positive influence on the team is to always be asking what you can do for the good of the team or for the good of a customer. If we focus there, we'll harness our potential and be aligned for success and high productivity!

If our team spirit is a function of constantly helping others, we'll likely cast aside egocentricities and thrive on positive results with and for others.

Your inclination to be a dynamic, contributing team member is also influenced by the environment in which you find yourself at work. That environment reflects the culture of the organization, and the culture is a result of the core values of management. Each element is key. The one thing WE know is that we can decide to be our best today. Attitude and commitment are choices we make. If the culture and core values of the organization are inconsistent with our beliefs, we made a mistake in accepting the job. That is why it is so important for leaders to put that information out front. Since a sense of mission and purpose is at the forefront of employee motivation, clarifying and reminding the team members what the company is about and what it stands for is of paramount importance.

When Francesco Molinari won the British Open Golf Championship, he played great and didn't get a single bogey the entire weekend! He was, as they say, in the *zone*. He was focused, unemotional, determined, and was performing at an extraordinary level. The only thing more impressive than someone in his/her zone of excellence is when the *entire team* is in the zone of excellence! This becomes a matter of leadership, morale, inspiration, and, of course, individual commitment.

We've all seen sports teams get there and accomplish a great victory together. Likewise, it is all predicated on each of us being committed to exceptional results for our team to prevail.

Remember, a chain is only as strong as its weakest link and a team is only as strong as its weakest member! Don't pull up the rear.

Lead the charge with a resilient attitude! Master the *power of a positive team spirit* and win like never before. Few things are more powerful than the contagion of a victorious leader!

YOUR LEADERSHIP MAKES THE DIFFERENCE

- Others see us as strong leaders when we make a positive impact on them. True leaders create an environment around team members which causes them to soar to new heights.

- The most skilled leaders impress others because they have a clarified vision and a plan to make it become a reality.

- "Find a positive way to say it and you will have an organization of higher morale". Og Mandino

- When leaders display a humble demeanor rather than an outsized ego, the team members are much more likely to be enthusiastic followers.

- If you want to stand out from the crowd, be a leader who is constantly looking for new innovations.

- Show your best self to others. When they see in you a combination of humility, optimism, and determination, you will have set a great example and made a positive impression.

 I recommend you
view this video clip:

"The Vision of A Leader"

https://vimeo.com/345565660

ABOUT THE
AUTHOR

Don Hutson's career spanning speaking, writing, consulting, and sales has brought him many honors. He worked his way through The University of Memphis, graduating with a degree in Sales. After a successful sales career, he established his own training firm and today is CEO of U.S. Learning based in Memphis, TN.

He has spoken to over half of the Fortune 500, is featured in over 100 training films, and currently addresses some 50 audiences per year. He is the author or co-author of fifteen books, including the number one *Wall Street Journal* and

New York Times bestseller, *The One Minute Entrepreneur* (with Ken Blanchard).

Don's knowledge and platform experience in selling value, leadership, and negotiations have been sought out by companies and associations throughout the world.

Don was on the Founding Board and is Past President of The Society of Entrepreneurs. He was also on the Founding Board and is Past President of the National Speakers Association, and the recipient of NSA's "Master of Influence" Award. He is a member of Speakers Roundtable, a think tank of twenty thought leaders in training and development. He is also in the Speakers Hall of Fame.

The Author's Services

Don Hutson and the team at U.S. Learning have decades of experience in training and educating sales and management professionals in many industries. In addition to his books, videos, and speaking appearances, Hutson and his company are pioneers in the production and marketing of online Training Programs on numerous business development topics now available online at www.USLearningVT.com.

All appearances are provided after an in-depth needs analysis, and are tailored to the needs and specific objectives of each client. The topical areas covered are:

- Basic and Advanced Sales Principles

- Negotiation Strategies

- Selling Value

- Entrepreneurship

- Leadership/Management

- Customer Loyalty

For an initial conversation or to set up an in-depth discovery meeting with Don, call 901-767-5700 or email him at Don@DonHutson.com. Visit our web site at www.DonHutson.com for more information.

Now, about your BONUS! First, thank you for purchasing *Standing Out From The Crowd*. For additional learning, please enjoy a FREE 7-day access into selected chapters of my Virtual Training Program, *SELL VALUE, NOT PRICE!* by visiting www.USLearning.com/SVbookbonus.

CPSIA information can be obtained
at www.ICGtesting.com
Printed in the USA
LVHW040852290819
629082LV00001BA/1

9 781949 033151